All the Pretty People

Tales of Carob, Shame & Barbie-Envy

By Ariel Gore

Illustrated by Summer Pierre

LIT STAR PRESS

ALL THE PRETTY PEOPLE:
TALES OF CAROB, SHAME & BARBIE-ENVY

©2011 by Ariel Gore

Published by LIT STAR PRESS

All rights reserved. Printed in the United States of America. No part of this book may be reproduced or transmitted in any form without written permission from the publisher or the author, except by a reviewer who may quote brief passages for the purpose of review.

Some of these stories have appeared in slightly different forms in *Spork, Red Room, Miriam's Well, The Sun, Santa Fe Literary Review, Best of Duke City Dimestories*, and maybe a couple of other places I can't remember.

First edition, First printing: March, 2011
ISBN 10: 1-934620-12-1
ISBN 13: 978-1-934620-12-0

Cover and book design by Ariel Gore
Illustrated by Summer Pierre

Printed in Portland, Oregon by Eberhardt Press
Distributed by Microcosm: www.microcosmpublishing.com

In this pleasing, contrite wood-life which God allows me, let me record day by day my honest thought without prospect or retrospect, and, I cannot doubt, it will be found symmetrical, though I mean it not, and see it not. My book should smell of pines and resound with the hum of insects. The swallow over my window should interweave that thread or straw he carries in his bill into my web also. We pass for what we are.

—R.W. Emerson

ALSO BY ARIEL GORE

Bluebird: Women and the New Psychology of Happiness
Portland Queer (editor)
How to Become a Famous Writer Before You're Dead
The Traveling Death and Resurrection Show: A Novel
Atlas of the Human Heart
Whatever, Mom
The Mother Trip
The Hip Mama Survival Guide

All the Pretty People

This is a book about all the pretty people I used to know in California. A book about wanting to be one of those pretty people and never quite knowing how. I mean, we didn't have a television. *How was I to know that all the pretty people got their answers from TV?*

"We pass for what we are," Emerson said. I never passed for one of the pretty people, but I passed for other things. I guess I didn't understand why all the wrong people looked so pretty.

Part One: The '70s
(which mysteriously stretch into 1981)

first sounds

It's all dark. The converted garage where I live with my mother and my sister. Just sound: My father's voice, high-pitched and manic, his fist banging on the back door. My father out in the dark and warm night, violating a restraining order, ranting about Catholic priests and banana splits.

I peer around the door frame from the living room into the tiny kitchen, hoping to catch a glimpse of my father when my mom opens the door. But she doesn't open the door. She just stands there, a shadow, hands on her head.

I tip-toe back through the living room, Carole King singing her *Tapestry* from the turntable. I tip-toe into the bedroom I share with Leslie. She rocks herself back and forth on the top bunk.

"Don't worry," I tell her as I crawl into the bottom bunk. "It's just our crazy dad."

In the light of morning, my mother holds a black, hardbound sketchbook. Her fingernails painted red. She opens to the first page, to my author photo, to the title: *Stories by Ariel Gore*. "Do you want to write a story, tiniest?"

I nod. I don't know how to write yet, so I sit next to my mother at the round wooden table and I dictate my story, stringing words together like daisies in chain.

Little Red Riding Hood
(1974)

The ocean shone white and blue
While Little Red Riding Hood was watching it.

The sun was almost to land on the ground.
Run, run, run, run.

Then she went home and her mother said,
"Take these cookies to your grandma."

Then she met a wolf.
But it wasn't a wolf, it was her Daddy.

It's simple like that. My story exists. No editing. No rewriting. It's not a good story or a bad story, not worthy or worthless.

No one has yet told me that girls shouldn't write or that white people have already written too much. All the ways we silence each other. It's just a story—told and recorded.

I imagine my book moonlit.

cake

She's really skinny, my mom, but she's on a diet and the diet has rules. One rule is she can only eat our leftovers. Another rule is she can only eat when she's standing up.

It's the '70s and my mom has a perm. We call it a permanent even though it's not permanent. Normally my mom has straight hair.

Normally I have curly hair, but my mom puts cream on it and holds the hot blow dryer close to my scalp and combs through it with a purple plastic comb and after half an hour it's almost like straight.

It's the '70s and my mom reads *Vogue Magazine*, but she says "consumerism is a vacuum" and she won't let me or Leslie read magazines or watch TV because we might get sucked into the vacuum.

There's no getting out, once you get sucked in.

She named us Leslie and Ariel because she says those names are "androgynous." She says we'll pass for men on paper. "It's important to pass," she says.

It's the '70s and we live in a duplex—me and my mom and Leslie.

My Gammie Evelyn bought it for us, the duplex. She said it wasn't right, moving all the time, living in converted garages. "It's smart to have a duplex," my Gammie Evelyn says. "You can live in one side and rent out the other side and then you don't need a man." That's what my Gammie Evelyn says. "But, of course," my Gammie Evelyn says, "it's better to have a man." My Gammie Evelyn is pretty just like my mom, but she's not so skinny.

I'm not skinny, either.

My Gammie Evelyn whispers "that child is going to be obese," but my mom says it's just baby fat. I'll be skinny one day.

My mom wears tall, brown, high-heeled, zip-up boots and at the end of the day she clomps up the wooden porch stairs to our duplex. Inside, she sits on the black and white checkered sofa bed and she lifts her feet one by one and I unzip the boots and I pull them off.

My mom has a big brown leather purse with rhinestones that scrawl the shape of a dollar sign, but there isn't any money in that purse. When there is money in it, I steal it. I hide it under the little green couch in my doll house. It's my mad money. "It's always important to have mad money." That's what my Gammie Evelyn says.

It's the '70s and Leslie is turning eight. That means I'm five. My mom buys us a carob cake with white icing and an androgynous plastic figurine on top. We want that cake. We've been eyeing that cake all day. Normally, we're not allowed to eat sugar. Not any. And that carob cake has lots of sugar in it. We know it does. Finally, as the August sky outside our kitchen window turns a darker blue, my mom lights a candle on the cake and she nods and says, "Go ahead," and Leslie blows out the flame and we go at that cake with our hands. We just dig right in and mush it up and spread the carob and the white icing all over the round wooden table.

The sugar tastes good.

Later, my mom will eat the mushed-up carob cake and white icing out of a blue bowl while she's standing up.

the priest

The priest is supposed to be a secret.
The front door opens and the floorboards creak after we've gone to bed.
If he's still here in the morning, asleep on the black and white checkered sofa bed, we can't tell anybody.

The priest looks ancient to me, deep laugh lines around his eyes, bald on top except for a wispy tuft of hair that sticks straight up in the middle. In my illustrations of The Last Supper, Jesus is the priest and he's a smiling pumpkin head—his tuft of hair becomes a green-brown vine.

We've never been Catholic before but now we go to morning Mass and afternoon Mass and we wash our sins away in the silver bowl of holy water at the entrance to St. Ann's Chapel. Now we take and eat, this is the body of Christ. Now we take and drink, this is the bittersweet blood of Our Savior.

How can he save us if he's dead?
Nobody knows.

The priest wears a long white robe and a hippie tie-dyed stole that hangs around his neck like a scarf. When everyone stands to recite the Lord's Prayer, I stare up at the stained glass crucifixion scene. *Ourffffatherwhoartinheaven...* I move my lips to remember the sounds, but I keep silent. Then we all trace triangles from our

that lingers in the air. "Is that God?"

"Yes," the priest says. He's dressed now, replacing the cushions on the sofa.

I think maybe the priest has a bright flame hidden behind his eyes because his whole face glows when he smiles. So I have it. God is a triangle. "Why don't you wear a black priest suit?"

The priest is wearing a cardigan sweater like Mr. Rogers. I've seen Mr. Rogers on my Gammie Evelyn's TV.

"I was never terribly comfortable in my cassock," the priest says. "Haven't worn it for years."

"Did Adam and Eve have bellybuttons?" I ask the priest, lifting my shirt to show him mine.

He pulls his socks on, clucks his tongue. "Well—*ha*—the Bible doesn't say, but most of the art shows them looking like normal people."

"Normal people with bellybuttons?"

But before the priest can answer me, the doorbell rings and my mother comes rushing out from the bathroom—"shit"—pulling on the flowered dress that makes all the kids on the block call us Gypsies.

The priest stands up, confused, and I pushed him into our living room closet.

My mother nudges the front door open just a crack to see who's there.

Leslie shuffles in, rubbing her eyes. She climbs onto the couch, grabs the priest's glasses from the side table and slips them into the pocket of her Chinese robe. "Don't say anything stupid," she warns me.

"We're doing wonderfully," my mother is telling the person at the door. "Thanks so much for stopping by." I can tell my mother is trying to wrap up the conversation, but the lady outside keeps asking questions. "Oh, yes," my mother says. "The girls are still in their pajamas, but do come in."

The blue-haired lady from church follows my mother inside and wrinkles her nose at me when I hit my triangle. She wears a brown polyester dress and holds a big black purse.

My mother gestures toward our room, "The girls sleep in there..."

The lady doesn't say much, just sniffs around the corners of our duplex. My mother has already told me about the witch who tattled on the priest's brother when he was a priest, too. Witches come snooping after rumors and they tattle on the priests when they sneak out at night to see *Harold and Maude* and don't come back to their rooms until morning. I'm sure the blue-haired lady is a witch, with her big black purse and her pointy nose.

"It really was so sweet of you to stop by—" my mother is saying. "So sweet."

I think I hear the priest cough in the closet, so I give my triangle a good whack.

The blue-haired lady wrinkles her nose at me again. "Good day, then," she says. And we watch from the window as she drifts down the walkway, clutching her big purse.

My mother is laughing when she opens the closet door, but the priest looks rattled, his little tuft of hair askew.

Leslie hands him his glasses and he nods, smiles his bright jack-o-lantern smile, and slips out the back door.

It's smart to have a duplex with a back door.

let us pray

Sunday morning we dip our fingers in the holy water and wash our sins away. We've never been baptized, but the priest told me himself it doesn't matter. We were born pure and we're pure still.

The priest stands by the door of the church, wearing his long, white robe.

"Good morning, Father Duryea," the parishioners say as they file past.

The priest smiles at my mother.

She wears her red bandana and big gold hoop earrings.

"Good morning, father," I coo up at the priest.

"Good morning, Chickadee," he whispers.

We sit in a pew at the back of the church, me and my mom and Leslie.

A woman near the pulpit strums her acoustic guitar and sings "Moonshadow." Folk Mass.

Still, Jesus hangs on his cross in the stained-glass window, two women crying at his feet. His blood drips down from his palms like a warning: *Here's what can happen.*

"Let us pray," the priest begins.

And I pray to my triangular god that soon the priest will be my father for real.

visiting hours

My real father lives out by the San Francisco Airport, a half an hour from our duplex and St. Ann's Chapel. He lives in one of those big brown apartment buildings that's perpetually NOW RENTING, blue and white banner rippling in the wind.

We pull into the parking lot and Leslie and I climb out from the back seat of my mother's mustard-colored Vega. My mother walks us up the metal stairs to the apartment, exchanges a few calm words with my father, then she's gone.

My father closes the door, whispers "Goodbye, Catwoman."

Clutter and filth. Everything here is covered in a thin, sticky film. Greasy stove. Empty Coors cans filled with cigarette butts. Naked ladies in magazines. An unsteady pile of dirty dishes in the sink, remnants of canned soup congealing in a pot on the stove, and he talks about a job washing other people's dishes.

My father has pet mice, some black, some white, some spotted. He has dozens of them. They live in a doll house with black and white checked floor paper, tiny violins propped here and there, paper dolls, and doll-sized pots of food. The mice are forever knocking over the doll furniture.

Leslie and I sit at a square black table, sipping instant miso soup from Chinese bowls and watching the mice fight over sunflower seeds.

Dear Ariel,

Where are we in the universe?

I hear you have the mumps even though it's sunny. If I buy you a violin, will you play it? If I visit, will you come out to dance in the yard, or will that cunning witch Catwoman keep you hidden in the back room with a banana split?

Mother wants me to move back to Carmel. What do you think?

Love, Dad

Ariel Gore
650 Addison
Palo Alto, CA
94301

school

You know, before I went to school, I didn't know that you were supposed to have two parents—one mom and one dad both living with you in the same house with no stepparents and no grandparents. Lots of people didn't have that, but before I went to school I didn't know that the ones who did were better than us.

Before I went to school, I didn't know that you were supposed to eat meat sandwiches for lunch. Lots of people didn't eat meat sandwiches—they ate school lunches in the cafeteria or they ate avocado and alfalfa sprout sandwiches on whole wheat bread like we did, but before I went to school I didn't know that the meat sandwich eaters were better than us.

Before I went to school, I didn't know that you weren't supposed to draw pictures of your parents naked. The women in my mom's drawing group on Wednesday nights always drew naked pictures of the naked models, but when Ms. Pulisci gave us the paper and told us to trace the letters and write "*Mother can do it*" and draw a picture, nobody else in the whole kindergarten drew their mother naked.

window

Ms. Pulisci stands in front of me. Her tall, red beehive hairdo blocking my view of the chalkboard behind her.

The chalkboard is marked with letters.

I could read all those letters if Ms. Pulisci would just move her hairdo.

Ms. Pulisci is my kindergarten teacher. She lives faraway in Burlingame and she likes ladybugs. She wears ladybug buttons and ladybug shirts and ladybug scarves.

I'm sitting on the rough green carpet, running my hand over it, wondering if Ms. Pulisci knows that the guy outside the window with the long curly Louis XIV wig is my crazy dad.

I wonder if the kids know. I think they all know.

I wonder when he'll go away.

The florescent lights flicker and everything flickers grey pink white.

I gaze out the big window, past the guy in the wig. I look at the buildings across the street, at the housing project where Sonja Carson and Janelle Santo get to live. The housing project where there are no fathers.

At the end of the block, there's my dad's white truck. I'm pretty sure everybody knows.

I scoot around real slow, until I'm facing the other window.

vacation

I'll tell you a secret. We're going on vacation. Me and my mom and Leslie and the priest. It's a secret vacation. We wake up early in the morning and we drive in the priest's green Dodge Dart. We drive and we drive.

"What town are we in?" I want to know.

"We're in no town," the priest says.

"Why's it so hot?" I want to know.

"Because we're in the middle of the state," the priest says.

We pass dusty fruit stands and tired wooden houses where white children play in dirt yards. We drive until the road narrows and winds up out of the valley and into the mountains.

"What town are we in now?" I want to know.

The priest winks at me in the rear view. "This is the high Sierra."

And we drive and we drive up into that high Sierra until the priest finally pulls over on the side of the highway and we climb out. We strap green canvas packs onto our backs and we walk, ducks in a row, following the priest along a footpath to the shore of the secret lake. We take off our shoes, wade in toward a wooden canoe. Cold and urgent blue, that high Sierra lake.

We pile into the canoe and we paddle with big wooden paddles for a long time. We paddle until we get to a secret cabin that the priest's parents built a long time ago.

"Were you parents pioneers?" I want to know.

The priest laughs at that. "My father was a wood carver," he says. "My mother was an opera singer." He hesitates, scratches his chin. "Actually, my father was an architect. But there wasn't any work in the 1930s, so he carved wood and he built things."

In the secret cabin there are wood carvings and white candles stuck in empty wine bottles and old canvas sleeping bags and checkers games and mosquito repellent.

Outside, there's a circle of stones. "Come down here," the priest says. "We have to build a campfire before night falls."

And we build the fire with kindling sticks and logs. We roast marshmallows. The priest says we're supposed to hold the marshmallows near the hot orange coals of the big logs and wait until the outsides turn golden brown, but it's quicker if you just light the marshmallow on fire and then blow it out and peel the black part off and eat the middle.

I'm eating the sweet middle of a marshmallow when I realize it's suddenly dark. I look up: a hundred stars? A thousand? The longer I watch, the more stars appear. Layer upon layer of stars. "Too many stars," I whine, disoriented.

"You can make a wish," my mom tells me.

"It's good luck if you see a shooting star," Leslie says. "Look."

"What happens when a star falls out of the sky?" I ask the priest, but he shakes his head. "Those stars are so far away, their light takes so long to travel to your little eyes, those stars have long-since burned themselves out."

"The stars are gone already?"

"Burned out," the priest nods.

But I know the priest is wrong this time. The stars whisper in my ear. They whisper, *we're not dead*. And the stars whisper, *don't just make one wish*. They whisper, *All things are possible*.

My mother rests her head on the priest's shoulder.

I think I like it here. I like my stars.

Archdiocese of San Francisco
Chancery Office
445 Church St.
San Francisco, CA 94114

4 June 1976

Dear Mr. Duryea:

   It is with deep sorrow that I am obliged to notify you that by attempting marriage you have incurred the automatic excommunication provided in Canon 2244 of the Code of Canon Law. In addition to the suspension which you have already received, under Canon 2244 you will be automatically excommunicated. Consequently, you are forbidden to celebrate Holy Mass or to receive Holy Communion.

   We have been saddened by the fact that many people are scandalized at St. Ann's Chapel when they see you approach the holy table. I hope that you will respect the provisions of the law of the Church and not place any priest who is celebrating Mass under the disagreeable obligation of refusing you Holy Communion.

   Despite our sorrow over this situation, I assure you that we will keep you in our prayers, with the hope that through the grace of God you may be restored to full membership in the church and priestly activities, through your obedience to the laws of the church.

Yours sincerely in Christ,
Joseph T. McGucken
Archbishop of San Francisco

June 7 1976

Dear Mr McGucken,

   Your letter, graciously timed to arrive on my wedding day, was so remote from the reality of the occasion that it could hardly arouse anger, much less fear. It reads like a document disinterred from the age of the Inquisition, complete with stifling legalism, muted threats, and crocodile tears. I ask you to consider which spirit is represented by such a letter: the spirit of Christ, or that of the Pharisees?
   Your anxiety over scandal at St. Ann's appears to be unwarranted. Some 500 people attended my "attempted" marriage in the Stanford Memorial Church. Most of them were practicing Catholics, and they made their warm support very evident.
   I will continue to minister in all available ways, and my conscience is entirely clear in doing so. I am and will remain a priest; that is why I did not go through the procedure of laicization. I do not wish to be a layman. And I do not intend to admit the rightness of the law which denies the option of Christian marriage to priests. There are countless Catholics--I meet them daily--who are alienated by the rigidity and inhumanity of the official church and its representatives. I am finding a fruitful ministry among them.
   Despite the hollow booming of your Automatic Canons, I am peacefully in communion with the universal Church, and shall receive communion when I please. If priests are too intimidated, I am sure the lay minister will not be.

Sincerely yours,
John S Duryea

owl

I have an owl. My owl lives in my oak. My oak lives outside my bedroom window. I have my own bedroom now.

After my mom married the priest, we gave our duplex back to Gammie Evelyn and we moved into a big Spanish house that the priest's father built. It has stucco walls and a red-tile roof.

I've never seen my owl, but my owl talks to me at night.

My owl says it's OK to be quiet.

My owl says it's OK if people don't see you.

Leslie says I don't have any owl. She says her bedroom's right next to my bedroom so if I've got an owl she'd hear it, too.

My mom says I don't have any owl. Probably not, anyway. Her bedroom's right next to my bedroom on the other side and she hasn't heard any owl, either.

My stepdad, John, says maybe I have an owl. "I've never heard an owl out there," he says, "but it might be there. It might be a Great Horned Owl. Or maybe even a Screech Owl. An owl might live up in that old oak. I wouldn't doubt it."

I don't think my owl has horns. And I know my owl doesn't screech. John says owls are nocturnal.

Sometimes I dream my owl comes into my room. I pet my owl behind its ears and my owl sits with me. My owl says it's OK to go crazy sometimes, but it's best not to stay crazy.

don't tell catwoman

At recess Leslie comes rushing up to me. I'm hanging on the monkey bars but she rushes right up. "Dad's here," she breathes, half-scared, half-excited.

Back in my classroom, I sharpen pencils and try to sneak glances out the side window. When the bell finally rings, I rush out to the curb, expecting to find my dad sitting in his truck, expecting to climb into the back and drive away, but he's nowhere along the curb, nowhere in the parking lot.

I walk along Addison Avenue looking down, trying not to tread on too many cracks, one step in each square so I won't break my mother's back. My patent leather Mary Janes are scuffed and rain-worn. The straps pass through the buckles and curl up at the ends. When I turn left on Waverly, that's when I hear it: The sound of the off-key trumpet belting out the notes of a tune I don't recognize. I look up, and there he is, sitting cross-legged in the back of his white Toyota pick-up parked across the street from the big Spanish house where me and my owl live. He's wearing a paint-splattered yellow windbreaker and his Louis XIV wig. And he's blowing red-faced into that trumpet. "Dad!" I go running across the street without looking either way. "Dad!"

He lowers his trumpet and smiles. "Don't tell Catwoman I was here."

carmel

Mornings in Carmel, Grandpa woke up early. I listened from the back bedroom as he ran his bath water and splashed around in the tub with his hand-held shower head. Then he'd hop back across the hallway and into his bedroom to put on his leg.

By the time I got up, brushed my teeth and tip-toed into the living room, Grandpa was all dressed in his clean tweeds, sitting in his leather armchair and reading *The Wall Street Journal.*

"G'morning, Grandpa," I'd pipe up.

He paused, fold his paper and set it on the table next to him, swing his chair around to face me. "Well, good morning, Ariel."

He stood up by pushing a button on the side of his knee (it made a quick mechanical exhaling sound, like a bus just before it starts moving). Then he walked his slow, uneven walk into the kitchen ahead of me.

"Well, hello there, Ariel," Grandma smiled as she sets out our cereal bowls. "What will you take?"

Grandpa took Grape-Nuts and liked his eggs poached.

I took raisin bran and liked my eggs sunny-side up because that sounded the prettiest and no one at my mom and stepdad's house in Palo Alto ever asked me how I took my eggs.

When Leslie was with me in Carmel, she took raisin bran and no eggs. But first she went for a jog on the beach. Sometimes she missed breakfast with Grandpa. Sometimes she missed the whole trip—something about our crazy dad in the basement apartment, something about it all making her too sad, something about dreams and tears and nightmares and Leslie being too sensitive for her own good, something that got discussed after I went to bed, something that, when it did come up before I went to bed, inspired me to yawn and say, "Whew, big day! I'm tired," and leave the room because I already had it all worked out—who I was in Carmel with my grandparents and my dad and who I was in Palo Alto with my mom and stepdad—I had a system and I didn't want to be a part of any discussion that might mess up my system.

"It's quite immoral to abandon the father of your children and marry a Catholic," Grandma said.

Most people thought my mom shouldn't have married John because he was a priest, but for my grandmother it was bad enough that he was Catholic.

"It's a shame about your hair, Ariel," Grandma said.

I thought to tell her that she could fix it, my hair, with the cream and the hot blowdryer close to my scalp. But my grandma was on to a new topic now. I would let my hair go curly in Carmel. With each passing day in Carmel, my hair got curlier.

"You know you're living under the poverty level in Palo Alto, don't you?" Grandma muttered.

I pretended not to hear her.

Grandpa took a spoon full of Grape Nuts.

"I've already eaten," my grandma said.

A yellow and white magnet on the fridge warned: "You can never be too rich, too thin, or have too many silk blouses."

We all smiled at each other and then we turned to watch *Good Morning America*.

Imagine. A TV in the kitchen. In Carmel, we had a TV in every room. And TVs weren't the only difference.

In Palo Alto, we were liberal Democrats. We had Amnesty International meetings in our living room and we believed in a compassionate God, outsider art, harmless ghosts who came to dinner, and whole grain bread from the BriarPatch Co-op market where my stepdad worked.

In Carmel, we were conservative Republicans. We thought President Carter was a peanut-farming embarrassment and we knew that the only way to peace was a powerful army. The military budget mattered to us personally, after all. Grandpa had co-founded one of the largest defense and intelligence corporations in the world. "It's the reason we're so comfortable," Grandma chirped when I asked her about it. The other reason we were so comfortable was that Grandma's father had a copper mine up in Anaconda, Montana, and a few more down in Chile, where Grandpa was born. There was a scuffle over those mines, the ones in Chile. When Salvador Allende took over, he said those mines belonged to the people. But lucky for the Anaconda company, the American government went down there and set it all straight—switched out Allende for Pinochet. But Grandma didn't talk so much about Pinochet—or about Anaconda. She talked about Grandpa. He'd had bone cancer as a kid, had his leg amputated, but that didn't stop him from becoming a fine lawyer. He was invited to work on the atom-bomb, you know, but Grandpa said, *atom-bomb—bah!* He had grander aspirations. My grandpa dreamed of making a bomb that could harness all the power of the sun.

In Palo Alto, we did not believe in bombs. We thought they were destructive. And we boycotted grapes and all things Chilean because we thought it was messed up that the U.S. government would overthrow a democratically-elected socialist guy like Allende. And we took it personally because my stepdad's old friend had been disappeared down there. I didn't understand quite what that meant, *to be disappeared*, except that it was slightly different than simply disappearing. Nothing like the difference between shooting and getting shot, but more like the difference between sinking and getting sunk. It suggested the presence of a force outside oneself. In Palo Alto, we followed news of people's revolutions around the world and discussed liberation theology over dinner.

In Carmel, we followed the stock market and we lunched at The Golf Club, which we call The Club, not to be confused with The Beach Club, which we call The Beach Club.

When my mother packed us off to Carmel, she gave us two instructions:

1) Don't get in the car with your father.
2) Order the most expensive thing on the menu.

The most expensive thing on the menu at The Club was Fresh Monterey Bay Shrimp Louis. $13.95. The Crab Louis was $13.50, so I never tries it. I ate Shrimp Louis every day for 14 days out of every summer, every day for 14 days out of every winter, every year for seven years out of my childhood.

Once, on the way home from The Club in my grandparent's red Jaguar, I asked "Why do we eat at The Club every day?" I was thinking the most expensive thing on the menu someplace else might be steak or linguini with clam sauce and as much as I liked Monterey Bay Shrimp Louis, I wanted to try something else.

"Why do we eat at The Club every day?" Grandpa repeated after me.

"Why do we eat at The Club every day?" Grandma repeated.

"Why do we eat at The Club every day?" Leslie chimed in, eyes wide and expectant. She had food on her mind, too. I could tell.

"Yes, why do we eat at The Club every day?" I asked again.

The silence that followed made me wonder if I hadn't said something terribly wrong, but I wasn't sure how to take it back.

"Well," Grandpa finally offered as we speed past a golf course. "Because that's the kind of people we are."

basement

The basement of the old Spanish house in Palo Alto is small and dark. Just a closet of a basement, really. I spend hours down here with my flashlight, digging through boxes and trunks. The priest's Christening gown is down here, the frilly white dress that's yellowing. I can't believe a baby boy would ever wear a dress like that. I can't believe the priest was ever a baby, small and soft.

I set my flashlight up on a shelf and I let it shine down on me like a spotlight. I try on the priest's mother's wedding dress over my blue shorts and T-shirt. She must have been tall, the priest's mother.

I take out the priest's old stuffed animals, too, Mama Bow and Papa Bow and Baby Bow. I set them up in a row on top of the old trunk. I'm a lady getting married and I have three little dogs. The cement basement floor is cold on my bare feet and I think, *that's how life was in the olden days.* Cold feet.

I peel the dress off and fold it carefully. I gather the stuffed animals and pack everything neatly into the trunk.

I can be very quiet.

Quiet like I'm not even here.

I have to stand on two boxes to reach the priest's mother's Ouija board up on the highest shelf. I climb down with it carefully, take the board from its box and set it in the center of the small open space on the cold floor. The board has all the letters of the alphabet and "YES," and "NO," and "FAREWELL."

I take the little heart-shaped wooden thing from the box, and set it on the Ouija board. The heart-shaped thing has a little round window in it, and three wooden pegs for legs. I place my fingers on it.

The priest says that spirits talk to people through Ouija boards. I think maybe the priest's mother wants to talk to me. Maybe other ghosts and spirits want to talk to me, too.

I sit on the cold floor, my hands on the heart-shaped thing, and I wait. I close my eyes. I concentrate. Very slowly, the heart-shaped thing begins to move. It moves so slow I wonder if it's really moving. Maybe I'm pushing it somehow. I want it to move. Maybe my desire moves it. But then the thing starts moving faster. Surely I'm imagining. I open my eyes. But it's dark down here. I can't see what the spirits are telling me.

neighbors

The Gilmans are our next-door neighbors and there are a lot of them. Annie Gilman is an only child but she has a mom and a dad and two aunts and a whole bunch of cousins. Her grandpa lives in a silver Airstream trailer in the driveway. The Gilmans have a lot of dead koi fish in their fish pond. I can't go over there after 5:30 p.m. anymore because that's when Annie's dad gets home from work and he says he's going to call the police on me and have me arrested for stealing their mail. He has short black hair and the name sewn onto his greasy blue work shirt is *Dick*.

I worry about when the police will come for me.

When the police finally show up in front of the Gilmans' house with their flashing red and blue lights but no sirens, I watch from the roof of our garage as two officers march up to the Gilman's porch. I figure they're probably getting all the details from Mr. Gilman about how I stole the mail and pretty soon they're going to come and arrest me. I wonder if I should climb back down the side of the garage and in through my bedroom window so I can pack my purple cords in my overnight backpack for jail, but I just sit there, watching. My owl watches, too. But when the policemen come back down the walkway, I'm confused, because it's Mr. Gilman who they have in handcuffs and it's Mr. Gilman who ducks into the backseat of their police car.

 I wonder if Mr. Gilman steals mail, too.

 The next day, Annie isn't at school. But her cousin Bobby says that Mr. Gilman is a child molester, which means I don't know what.

on the other side

Our neighbor on the other side is Anne White. Her house is bigger than ours but the same white stucco and red tile roof.

Anne White is old. She doesn't let us play in her pool. I stand in our backyard and I peer through the hole in the fence at the still turquoise water of Anne White's pool.

Anne White's brother lives in the attic apartment of her big house. He's an engineer but he doesn't have a job. He went to Stanford. He keeps his windows covered with tin foil. He wears a tin foil hat when he goes out, which is hardly ever. He says the tin foil keeps them from contacting him.

He doesn't say who "them" is.

chameleon

Pets are the best.
    Mom got us a new pet. She got us a chameleon. A chameleon is not a cuddly kind of pet. A chameleon looks like a lizard and it lives in a glass box called a terrarium with rocks on the bottom and a little piece of wood like its own little log. A chameleon can change colors to hide from predators. I want to name our chameleon Rainbow, but Leslie wants to name it Leon.
    I want to pet it!
    The top of the terrarium is glass just like the walls.
    Leslie wants to pet it, too.
    We want to see if our chameleon will change colors if we pet it. We have to be careful, opening the top.
    Leslie's more careful than me, so she starts to open the top and I reach to help her because we're going to pet our new chameleon and see if its skin is soft or scaly and Leslie says, "hey," and I don't know what happens next but it's quick like that, like *hey*, but it's bad because we drop the terrarium top and the chameleon scampers out of the way and my mother yells from across the room, "you could have killed it!" And I feel hot on my face but the chameleon is OK. We didn't kill him. We didn't even hurt him. Not at all. He scampered away. He's smart, our chameleon. And fast. Me and Leslie are scrambling to get the top back on.

It's OK if we can't pet the chameleon right now.

But my mom's grabbing us by the hair and she's dragging us away from the terrarium and out of the living room and into the dining room and now we're standing up against the wall and she's still got us by the hair and she says, "do you know what that would feel like if that glass lid fell on you? Do you know?" And she's still got us by the hair so she yanks our two heads in different directions and then all of the sudden she slams our two heads together, *bash!*

The first time she bashes our heads together it hurts a lot, like my skull might crack. Like a walnut. Cr-*ack*. She holds tight onto our hair, so the pulling hurts too—stings like. She yanks our heads in opposite directions again and I know she's going to bash them together again and I take a quick inhale to get ready for it, but then.

Something.

Magical. Happens.

Something. *Whoosh.*

It happens so fast nobody knows it happens.

The twilight changes from orangish to bluish outside and the part of me that my mother can see is still standing in front of her, next to Leslie, in front of the wall, but the important part of me isn't there anymore. The important part of me stands behind my mother, just watching over her shoulder, watching the girls against the wall. As their heads collide, I flinch. It looks like it hurts. Like cr-*ack*. And I feel sad for the girls when they cry. And I feel embarrassed for the one who is me. And I feel angry at Rainbow Leon the chameleon. Because he didn't get hurt. Not even at all.

muffy mcpherson

Muffy McPherson lives across the street. Her house has two stories and a swimming pool in the back yard. Muffy McPherson has a pink canopy over her bed and a Barbie Dream House under her bedroom window.

In her back yard, behind the pool, Muffy McPherson has a big red playhouse with a Barbie oven in it. We wear red and white checkered aprons and we pretend to make chocolate chip cookies. When we're done we go inside and Muffy McPherson's mother has made us real chocolate chip cookies that cool on a tray on an island in the middle of the kitchen. That's what it's called when you have a counter in the middle of your kitchen that you can walk all the way around—an *island*.

Muffy McPherson doesn't come over to my house to play and I'm glad—my mother wouldn't make us cookies and if my stepdad did, they'd have carob chips that he bought in bulk from the BriarPatch Co-op market and then he might take out his teeth.

Muffy McPherson's mother wears a lavender leisure suit and she uses real chocolate and she never takes out her teeth. Muffy's father goes to work in the morning and doesn't come home until dinnertime.

Muffy McPherson is in love with Harrison Ford.

It's not a crush. It's true love.

"I'm going to marry him," she says. And she dances across her pink-canopied bed, swishing her straight blonde hair back and forth.

My hair is dark and curly and I know there's not much I can do about it, but I think maybe if I had a pink canopy over my bed, I wouldn't feel so scared all the time.

"I have a poster of Harrison Ford," I tell Muffy.

"You do?" She stops moving, stares at me.

"Yeah," I say. "You can have it." I shrug, cool as I know how.

She nods real slow and I can't believe I actually have something Muffy McPherson wants. It makes me feel calm and powerful at the same time, like maybe we're not so different, Muffy and me. Like maybe even with my hair, I can be one of the pretty people when we go back to school in September.

The next day I come back with my poster of Harrison Ford, rolled up all nice. It's not actually my poster, I stole it from Leslie, stole it right off her wall, but I've already practiced my denial, practiced the blank look on my face when I'll claim I don't know what happened to the poster.

Muffy McPherson's mother answers the door and calls upstairs to Muffy. I bound up those soft stairs, close the door to Muffy's room behind me and begin to unfurl the poster.

Muffy McPherson's face is all thrill at first, but then she frowns. "That's not Harrison Ford," she scowls, then squints her eyes at the picture. "That's. Some. Old Man!"

"It isn't?" I look at it. Harrison Ford. The guy who's Doctor Doolittle in the movie.

Muffy McPherson clenches her teeth and crosses her arms and shakes her head, her hair swishing a little. "That's *Rex* Harrison. It says so right there." She points her thin finger to the signature at the bottom corner of the poster. "REX Harrison," she says again. "Are you *stupid?* Do you know even know who Harrison Ford is?"

I look at the poster, at Rex Harrison with his side burns and sly smile, and then at Muffy McPherson with her long blonde hair and stern look. I roll up the poster. I glance at the Barbie Dream House behind Muffy and I already miss playing with the Ken doll. I swallow hard. I say, "Yeah, I know who Harrison Ford is. I just. I was only kidding." And I feel something in the back of my throat that's hot and sore, like a coal from the campfire that got stuck there. And I don't know who Harrison Ford is.

I don't know who Harrison Ford is.

birds

The birds on the phone line outside the schoolroom just sit and watch. They wait. They watch through the window. Through the fog. They wait 'til more birds come. Wait 'til there are so many of them some silent voice tells them *1-2-3 go* and they alight all at once and even the black squirrels watch in awe as the birds swoop—all of them at once— *swoop*—as one— *swoop*—this way— *swoop*—that way. I want to be one of those birds. Watching and waiting. No one ever makes the birds talk. My mom calls me "owl child." Says I just watch, wide-eyed. Says I don't talk. She doesn't say it's a bad thing, being an owl child, but it seems like everybody else talks. Some people talk a lot.

"Ariel?" Miss Nissen's little nose is right up in my face and she's saying my name like it's a question. "Ariel?" She squints. She's blocking my view of the birds. "You're not paying attention, Ariel. What did I just say?"

"You said I'm not paying attention."

All the kids in the classroom laugh and Miss Nissen looks angrier, but it wasn't meant to be funny. That's what she said.

"What are you *doing*, Ariel?"

"I'm watching the birds."

But now the birds are gone and I'm writing *I will not watch the birds when I am supposed to be paying attention* over and over again while everyone else is outside playing dodge ball.

minnie wong

At lunch time, Minnie Wong and I shoplift candy bars from Channing Market. I like Butterfingers. She usually gets Three Musketeers. Then we walk to her house and we eat sweet and sour chicken drumettes over white rice in her darkly curtained kitchen.

We eat our candy bars and watch *All My Children* on TV.

Minnie Wong doesn't brush her hair.

Minnie Wong yells at her brother in Cantonese.

Minnie Wong teaches me to shave my legs with a kitchen knife.

She shares a little bedroom with her mother and her brother and a strange colorized plate that pictures the father they left in his coffin back in Hong Kong.

"I just remember my mother crying and crying," Minnie says as she chews on her Three Musketeers bar

"Why did you come to America?" I want to know. Hong Kong seems excellent and far away and exotic.

But Minnie says, "for a better life, *duh*. America."

Minnie's mother had been a nurse back in Hong Kong, but she couldn't pass the nursing tests in English, so now she works cleaning up piss at the convalescent hospital down the street.

America.

san francisco

Jim Jones was a priest like my stepdad, but then he went crazy like my real dad and now lots of people are dead. They're dead in Guyana and that's far away in South America.

But lots of them are from California. They are people from John's old church in Palo Alto and they are people from the communes near Carmel and they are people from the Jim Jones church up north.

Harvey Milk is dead, too. We hear it on the radio. A woman is saying that Mayor Moscone has been shot and killed and Supervisor Harvey Milk has been shot and killed and the suspect is supervisor Dan White and I am in the back seat of my mother's mustard-colored Vega and we are driving north from Palo Alto to San Francisco because everybody is dead.

That's what happens when you believe in God and men.

That's what happens when you're a famous priest or politician on TV.

That's what happens when you draw peace signs and grow things in your garden.

You die. They kill you.

And now there are candles everywhere. A parade of candles. Candles and candles all the way up Castro Street and the men who carry them all have mustaches.

It's cold in San Francisco, but it doesn't rain.

reina mendoza

Reina Mendoza's father is a political prisoner in Bolivia and I think that is the coolest thing. We were sitting out on the cement playground, Reina and me, both of us wearing ponchos, but mine was blue and white and made of lamb's wool and hers' was brown and black alpaca.

"I'm going to Peru with my mom over winter break," Reina told me. "I might see my dad."

She didn't look at me when she talked. She scratched the cement with a stick and almost whispered, just watching her stick.

That night, I dreamed Reina Mendoza's father in a tiny cement prison cell on an island in a giant blue lake. I could see the whole scene like I was watching it from above. That dusty island surrounded by reeds, cactus jutting up at the shore. My view zoomed closer in and closer in, until I was right there. Reina's father had short, Indian hair and a dark scar on his cheek. He wore a bright white T-shirt, was blindfolded with a black bandana. A man carrying a gun and wearing fatigues led him out of his cell, out of the prison and along a dry dirt trail. They stopped near a stand of trees and the man with the gun took aim and shot Reina's father right in the head. I woke up with one of those soundless screams and slouched into the kitchen, still in my baseball shirt nightgown.

My mother stood over the kettle, waiting for it to boil, a bag of organic tea in hand, and I whined about Reina Mendoza's father.

"My God, Ariel." My mother dropped her tea bag and clutched her chest dramatically. She looked like a cross between Joan Baez and Susan Lucci from *All My Children*. "The giant lake, Ariel. That's Lake Titicaca on the Bolivia-Peru border. We must call this child's mother and tell her of your premonition."

I thought it was kind of funny to call a lake titty-caca, but Reina Mendoza was new at school and even though she was a year younger than me, I figured I had a pretty good chance of making friends with her and I sure didn't want my mother to call her mother and rant about some crazy premonition. I'd had a nightmare, that was it. "Mom, don't," is all I said.

But of course, Mom did. "Ms. Mendoza?" My mother stood in front of John's desk, gripping the receiver.

I stood by, biting my knuckles hard, trying to make them bleed.

My mother waived her hand, shooing me away. "Ms. Mendoza, this is Eve, Ariel's mother. Yes, our daughters go to school together. Yes, I'm afraid there *is* a problem…"

When I broke the skin on my thumb knuckle, the blood tasted like seaweed.

"Yes," my mother said again, pushing me out into the hall and closing the door.

I waited there, right by the door. I couldn't hear what my mother was saying.

But that's how we got here now: Me and my mom and Leslie and John and Reina Mendoza and Reina Mendoza's mother, who looks skeptical, all sitting in a circle on the floor in our high-ceilinged living room, all somber-faced, white candles lit and sandalwood incense burning, chanting, praying to the spirits of Lake Titicaca to save Reina Mendoza's father from certain and imminent execution.

if i went to school

"I don't feel well," I tell my mother. "I can't go to school today. I think I have a fever." I'm standing in the kitchen in my baseball shirt nightgown, trying to look feverish.

My mother places a manicured hand on my forehead. "You feel fine to me," she says. "Get ready for school."

"I had a dream," I say, opening my eyes wide and trying to look psychic. "I dreamed something bad would happen if I went to school."

My mother narrows her gaze, looks more serious now. "What did you dream, tiniest?"

I shake my head. "It was very *bad*," is all I say.

And my mother bites her lipsticked lip and nods and says, "well, you better stay home, then."

rolling thunder

John knows a man named Rolling Thunder. Rolling Thunder can make things happen. He can heal a skinned knee and he can make rain fall.

If Rolling Thunder is on his way to the library and he realizes that he left his reading glasses at home, he just concentrates really hard on those reading glasses. "He meditates," John says. And he imagines those glasses back home where he left them and then he imagines them where he needs them and then he checks his satchel again and there they are.

"That's spiritual power," John says.

Samantha on *Bewitched* can make things happen, too. I've seen *Bewitched* on Minnie Wong's TV, but I've tried and I can't make my nose wiggle the way Samantha makes her nose wiggle and anyway my nose is bigger than her's.

"Rolling Thunder is a medicine man," John says. "He's a shaman. He says there's no shortage of anything but human understanding."

I decide that I'm going to make things happen, too.

There's no shortage of anything but human understanding. I whisper to myself.

I'm going to learn to make things happen. To move things.

I wake up early, before anyone.

The house is quiet.

a fine day

My grandparent's house on the Carmel beach is so clean. A cleanliness that might not seem excessive if my dad's basement apartment wasn't such a rat's nest of half-finished drawings and books in Chinese and glossy porn magazines that all smell of turpentine. But that's the way his apartment is and my grandparents' house is soft and smells like English lavender soap.

In Carmel, Grandpa keeps a spare leg in his bedroom closet.

Leslie gathers seashells on the shore.

Grandma serves ham sandwiches without the crusts in yellow napkin-lined baskets.

Everything in that little house is yellow: The soft wall-to-wall carpeting, the couches and the loveseats and the armchairs, the patio furniture, the wallpaper in the kitchen and the bathrooms, the soft toilet seat covers, all the sheets and the comforters and the pillow cases, the kitchen counters, the handles on the cabinets, the dishes. More yellow dishes than could ever fit into the little yellow dishwasher.

I sit next to Grandpa at his great big wooden desk. "I'm never going to get married," I tell him.

And Grandpa says, "Then you'll have to work hard, and you'll have to learn how to write. Not just typing, but writing. If you want to be a lawyer or a famous doctor or a senator, any of those things, you'll have to learn how to write."

I say, "I want to be a translator. Chinese and English. Back and forth." So we sit at his desk, writing on yellow stationary, and Grandpa tells me, "if you want to be a translator, or anything you want to be, you'll have a fine time. And if anybody asks you any questions, you just say, 'I am innocent.' Remember that, and you'll have a fine time."

I repeat after Grandpa. "I am innocent."

And Grandpa chuckles and pats me on the back. "That's right," he says. "I am innocent."

Then we get up and I follow my grandpa into the living room and he says, "You'll have to learn to play golf."

And Grandma says, "golf is a fine game."

And so Grandpa teaches me to swing a golf club, with the little putting machine that makes a mechanical gulping sound as it spits golf balls out across the yellow carpet.

"You'll make a fine golfer, Ariel," Grandpa tells me, patting me on the back. "A fine golfer."

I want to be a fine golfer. I want to have a fine time.

"When can I see my dad?" I ask, quietly so as to let my grandparents pretend not to hear me.

"Tomorrow," Grandma promises.

"Tomorrow should be a fine day," Grandpa says.

Tomorrow comes and my excessively clean grandparents, like old-world gatekeepers at the entrance of my dad's basement cave, allow me to cross over and see my father—the only one in the family who never tries to make a case for himself, never tries to persuade me, never acts like he's on trial. I've made the trip from Palo Alto to Carmel, passed the tests that consist mainly of table manners and knowing what to say when, knowing whether to pick up the doily with the finger bowl or leave it on the dessert plate; I've made it down the brick stairs, through the garage, and down more brick stairs, and everything is different. My father smokes Marlboro Reds, sits in his old green upholstered armchair with the stuffing coming out at the back. I can say *hello* or not say *hello*. I can think he's kind or think he's crazy—he doesn't seem to have an investment one way or the other. I can take a sip from his can of warm Coors beer or I can spill the flavor packet when I try to make Top Ramen on his hot plate. He doesn't give a shit which fork is for salad because he didn't have any salad and he doesn't have any forks. He has chopsticks and little jars of seaweed and kim-chee. I can set my mug of Kool-Aid down without a coaster, I can set it on a *Penthouse Magazine* or right on the coffee table. I can paw through the animation he's been working on, draw a few frames myself if I want to. It's the story of a thin cat searching in vain through the dream of 12,000 years.

"What's he searching for?" I ask my dad.

"I don't know. A way out?"

"What's his name?"

"Well, let's see..."

"Let's call him Felix."

"Naw," my dad says.

"How about Rat Fink?"

"Naw. We'll call him Mao. We'll call the whole thing Mao's Journey Through the Dream of Twelve Thousand Years: A Humble Cat's Search for a Way Out."

"Not very catchy," I tell my dad. "Things ought to be catchy. Like The Adventures of Rat Fink."

My dad nods, picks up a black calligraphy pen and writes the title on one of his thin square pieces of animation paper:

Mao's Journey Through the Dream of 12,000 Years:
A Humble Cat's Search for a Way Out
Or
The Adventures of Rat Fink

invitation

Muffy McPherson has invited me to spend a week with her family at their summer home in Pajaro Dunes.
I am not at all sure I can impart to you the breadth and the depth and the sheer importance of this invitation.

I mean, sure, maybe Whitney Anderson who lived in the big white house on the corner had already refused Muffy's invitation. Maybe Janelle Santo couldn't go. Maybe Holly Green was going to camp that week. Maybe I was the very last person on Muffy McPherson's list. But here's the thing: I was on that list.

GLITCH: The first day I am to be at Muffy McPherson's family summer home in Pajaro Dunes is also the last day I am to be visiting my crazy dad at my grandparent's house on the Carmel beach.

SOLUTION, AT LEAST ACCORDING TO THE GROWN-UPS: On the appointed day, my grandmother will drive me to Muffy McPherson's family summer home in Pajaro Dunes. It's not that far away from Carmel.

GLITCH: When the appointed day arrives, my grandmother smiles and says, "your father can drive you." And I'm not supposed to get in the car with my father.

SOLUTION: I don't say anything because I hardly ever say anything.

But that's how I end up in the open bed of my dad's white pick-up truck, riding up highway one, my blue dress billowing in the wind, on my way to Muffy McPherson's family summer home in Pajaro Dunes.

When Muffy McPherson's mom meets us in the driveway, she looks pale and kind of horrified. I don't know if she's horrified because my dad is intrinsically horrifying or because I've obviously been on the freeway in the back of his truck and there's something alarming about that—about a kid in a truck bed on the freeway in 1979—or if it's something else. Still, Muffy McPherson's mom has beautiful manners and whatever it is that makes her look horrified, she brushes it off and smiles as if everyone who arrives in Pajaro Dunes comes in the back of a white Toyota pick-up driven by a muttering crazyman who's come from Carmel in a long and flowing mullet wig.

It's just the way people arrive in Pajaro Dunes.
No big deal.

And pretty soon my dad is gone and I'm ensconced in a world of McPherson.

Oh, I like it here.

We eat meat and vegetables at night and we eat cereal and eggs in the morning.

Mr. McPherson says "I like my meat *raaare*," and he roars like a lion and we laugh.

Mrs. McPherson and Muffy have straight hair, but Mr. McPherson has curly hair like me.

Muffy and me, we make up games. We are spies like Harriet. We collect clues in a Hello Kitty notebook.

We leave the main house and we close the sliding glass door

as quietly as we can. We hop along the cobblestone paths that connect the vacation homes. We play on the porches of the uninhabited places. We listen to the waves. Days become evenings. Evenings become nights. We like the way we can close the glass door silently. But we know we shouldn't disappear without word. "We are going to the quiet house," Muffy McPherson whispers loud to her father as we leave. And he folds down the corner of his newspaper and he looks at Muffy and he looks at me and he smiles and he says, "have fun."

That's what he says.

We close the glass door and we creep away. Across the McPherson porch and onto the little stone walkway. We hop the walkway. Muffy McPherson says, "Hop the walkway, hop, hop, hop the walkway," and I repeat after her, *hop, hop, hop the walkway*, hoping all the way.

Surely, come September, I will be one of the pretty people.
I will.
I will be.
I will be like Muffy.
But I will be me.

These are the words I whisper under my breath as I walk and hop. I will be. *I will be.*

We hop in circles on the deck of the uninhabited house. I follow Muffy. She follows me. I am wearing a blue dress with shorts underneath. Muffy is wearing cotton stripes.

We hop.
We hop a lot.
We finally hop home.
We are not worried. We are hoppers.

We're at the glass sliding door. We are grasping the handle. We are happy. We are the last moment of childhood happiness we will ever know, but we don't know that yet.

There is an energetic shift. We don't like it. But we're not really sure what it means. Something is wrong. *Is it?* We question ourselves. *Maybe there has been no shift.*

Muffy McPherson's dad charges toward the door even before we've opened it.

Muffy McPherson's mom is coming for us, too, but she's crying. She is "where have you been?"

We are *shrug. Point. Like-we-said.*

She is crying. "I have been looking all over the dunes for you!"

But the dunes are out the front door. And we were out the back door where Mr. McPherson *saw* us go. He forgot where we went. He told Muffy McPherson's mom the wrong door. And now he is not telling her the truth. He is not telling her that he made a mistake. That he pointed to the wrong door. Now he is yelling at us, too. *But we told you where we were going, Mr. McPherson.* Muffy doesn't seem convinced that the truth will set us free. *We told you where we were going, Mr. McPherson.* Muffy just looks scared. She doesn't try to talk our way out of it all. *Muffy*, I whisper. *Tell him!*

We told him where we were going.

But we are in the bedroom now. And Mr. McPherson is beating Muffy with his brown leather belt. The sound is loud and hollow and Muffy is small and Mr. McPherson is big.

He hits her with his belt again and again and I feel sorry and quiet because I don't know how to make him stop. He stands over me, silhouette in the moonlight that streams in through the window behind him and he says, "I would beat you, too, if you were my kid."

And I hate his curly hair.

And I hate his angry eyes.

And for the first time in my life I am glad I have the father I have, the one who never comes after you with a belt, the one who if you tell him one thing and he hears another thing he questions himself first—he doesn't question you—because he is crazy and you are not crazy. And I love my father. And I know my father. And for the first time in my life I don't want to be Muffy McPherson or any of the pretty people, even if they get pools in their back yards. And I want to go home.

I want to go home now.

fling

Reina Mendoza's big sister doesn't know who her father is and I think that's the coolest thing.

It seems like he must be black because Reina Mendoza's mom is white, and Reina Mendoza looks pretty much Mexican even though her dad's from South America, and Reina Mendoza's big sister has chocolate skin and ringlets for hair and wide, dark eyes. But beyond the black, she doesn't know.

I start saying, "Yeah, I don't know who my father is. My mom doesn't really remember." And with that I try to sort of fling my hair but it doesn't really fling, exactly, because when I asked the hairdresser on Waverly to cut it like Dorothy Hamill's bowl cut, she said OK, but she didn't tell me that Dorothy Hamill was pretty much out of reach if your hair was curly like Little Orphan Annie's and the collision of Little Orphan Annie and Dorothy Hamill is still working itself out on my head.

Anyway.

I fling my hair to the extent that it will fling, and with that quick gesture I feel what it might feel like not to know who your father is. And it feels like power.

It feels like freedom.

babysitter

Crystal is my babysitter. When Crystal babysits me she makes little cigarettes out of green leaves and the smoke smells like our old duplex and Crystal laughs. But Crystal doesn't always show up when it's time to babysit me.

When Crystal doesn't show up, her sister Harmony shows up instead.

Harmony has long, dirty blonde hair and she carries a comb in the back pocket of her Ditto jeans.

Harmony is younger than Crystal, but they're both old—maybe even in high school.

The first time Crystal doesn't show up, Harmony says it's because she got her period which means she has bloody eggs in her underpants, so I hope that never happens to me.

The second time Crystal doesn't show up Harmony is crying and she says they got into a fight with their mom.

"Are you hurt?" I ask.

Harmony says she isn't hurt, so I guess her mom or Crystal is the one who got hurt, and I wonder if we should call an ambulance to take them to Stanford Hospital.

The third time Crystal doesn't show up, me and Harmony walk the five blocks up Waverly Street, down Channing, and up Bryant to her house. She lives with just her mom and Crystal. She has a purple parachute all billowy on her bedroom ceiling and it feels magical in there, like we're camping, but we're warm. "Crystal started smoking cigarettes," Harmony tells me. "Not just grass." She leans back on her bed and looks up at all that purple. "And her boyfriend stole my mom's car."

I nod and try to look serious, like I understand the gravity of the situation, so that Harmony will know I'm mature and a good person to tell things to.

The last time Crystal doesn't show up, Harmony stands at our front door all red-faced. My mom and I just stand in the arch of the doorway, looking at her.

Harmony's breathless like she ran all the way over here from her house. "Crystal had to go to the mental hospital," she says.

My mom half-gasps and says "Oh my God," and she turns and grabs her keys from the dining-room table and rushes down the hall and she slams the back door behind her and starts up the car.

Harmony is shaking when she comes in, but pretty soon she calms down and her face doesn't look so red and we leave through the back door and we walk up Waverly Street and down University Avenue to Swensen's Ice Cream to get mint chip cones.

television intervention

People started giving us televisions.

People: Gammie Evelyn, Grandma Gore, John's brother's wife, Muffy McPherson's mom, even Ann White's crazy brother showed up in our Mexican-tiled entryway with a television.

It was like sponsor-an-Ethiopian except we were Californian and we ate sprouted grain bread every day—we were just media-starved, and I guess this was alarming.

It was like, *Have you heard about that family down on Lincoln Ave.?*

They don't have.

What?

My god!

We were poor in an increasingly rich town and we lacked for a lot of things. We would have gladly accepted new three-speed bicycles or hand-me-down purple coats. But people didn't seem to understand that this one particular lack, this lack of a television, was more philosophical than financial.

Commercialism was a vacuum, after all—my mother always said it—and that vacuum could suck us up.

Still, the televisions arrived.

Leslie and I sat in the high-ceilinged living room like Christmas orphans, welcoming the bright new boxes. We could watch *Little*

House on the Prairie and *Bewitched*. Imagine! We caught glimpses of things. I found out why kids on the playground sometimes said "Marcia, Marcia, Marcia!" and laughed even though no one was named Marcia. I learned what it would be like to come from the planet Ork and why the boys in the back row always said "Nano-nano." But alas and Nano-nano, my mother was not interested in our growing cultural literacy. She had other plans for our new televisions.

She poured water into the back of the first one that arrived and I think she was quite pleased when it made that strange fizzling sound before it went blank.

Leslie and I were watching PBS on the second television when my mother suddenly appeared swinging the crow bar, bashing the television, violently I thought, and crying as she bashed it, "commercialism!" It was strange because the PBS people were actually in the middle of a pledge drive. White people with bad hair talking on telephones. But my mother swung her crow bar and cried "commercialism" until the thing went quiet.

The third television was color. A full color TV that arrived on the first of July. Leslie and I couldn't believe our luck, but we were nervous, too. Leslie covered the back of the new color television with tin foil hoping, I guess, to protect it from water attack. We took turns with our ears pressed to the door. My mother was quite small and we figured that with the adequate lead time, we could protect the new color television from her wrath.

We had failed to think seasonally, however, and so it was that when my mother burst into our room holding a Roman Candle in one hand and a rocket-shaped thing called "pyro glyphics" in the other, we jumped back, unprepared. She lit both fireworks at once with a single match, shoved them into the back of the television as if she didn't even notice the tin foil, and yelled, "Run!"

The explosion was large enough and bright enough, apparently, because no one ever brought us another television.

innocence

After dinner in Carmel, we climbed into the back of my grandparents' gold Nissan and headed out along winding roads, up toward the 17-mile drive. Grandpa stopped abruptly every few miles to point out a golf course in the dark or to avoid hitting a deer.

The 17-mile drive: The scenic loop through Pacific Grove and Pebble Beach, but we drove it at nightfall.

As the moon rose, the quiet in the car was interrupted only by periodic and random one-liners from Grandpa. "It is written," he'd say. Or "I am innocent."

Sometimes Leslie told stories to fill the silences, but I just curled up and tried to go to sleep.

It was then—as I fell into half-sleep and Leslie surrendered to the quietness and Grandma opened the passenger seat front window just enough to let in a faint scent of eucalyptus that mixed with the smell of the car's new plastic and upholstery—it was then I began to learn the sins of my parents.

"In my day, when your husband was having a difficult time, you stood by him. You stayed with him and took care of him. You did not just leave him and take the children away," Grandma said. I didn't know if her words were directed toward anyone in particular, or to the night air, but no one answered her.

"I give him money every month, but I don't have to. It's a

waste of money, really. I could stop giving him money any time," Grandpa warned.

"He was offered a job at Disney, but he wanted to spend his time with you girls. If he'd taken the job at Disney, everything would have been fine," Grandma said.

"I send your mother money every month. I send child support. But I don't have to. It's a waste of money. I could stop sending the child support any time," Grandpa said.

"They should never have gone to Europe, but they thought it would be nice for you girls. If they hadn't gone to Europe, everything would be fine."

"He shouldn't have gone to Berkeley."

"Maybe if they'd gotten married."

"Those draft cards soaked in blood."

"He should have gone to Harvard."

"He could have married anyone."

"She should have stood by him."

"It is written."

"I am innocent."

"If it weren't for you girls."

macy's

We're standing at the counter at Macy's, clothes my mother calls "chic" piled on the counter. She hands over her Macy's card.

"You're going to look so chic," she has told me. "You know," she has told me, "when you put something on a credit card, it's free."

The cashier has too much make-up on. Her eyelashes are thick with black, her eyebrows just drawn lines of brown pencil. I stare steady up at her, but she doesn't look at me. I don't think the clothes in our pile are chic, but I guess they're better than the hand-me-downs from my sister and I guess we're buying them.

The cashier smiles at us, then frowns. Her lipstick is pale and makes her lips look missing. "Ms. De Bona," she says. "Just a moment."

My mother grabs my hand tight and her fingernails dig into my palm.

When the cashier comes back she's holding my mother's credit card with just two fingers, like it might be dirty. "Ms. De Bona," she says. "I'm afraid I'm going to have to cut up this card. Do you have another method of payment?"

My mother lets her fingernails dig into my palm again before she lets go. "No I don't have another method of payment." She hesitates, reaches for her Macy's card, but the woman holds the card close to her chest. My mother grabs my hand again and pulls me away before I can see the look on the cashier's orangy face.

The racks of clothes look like merry-go-rounds as we pass. And my mother says, "that woman has *problems*."

coffin

At lunchtime I notice my stepdad's bicycle parked across the street from Addison Elementary, at the funeral home on Middlefield, so I tug on my friend Jessica's sleeve and we head over. But John isn't there.

It doesn't seem like anyone's here.

Anyone but me and Jessica.

There are empty chairs on the cement floor and an aisle down the middle, like church, so we creep down the aisle and we have to stand on our tip-toes to see who's in the coffin.

It's Anne White in her coffin. White, white Anne White who was my next-door neighbor. Anne White in her coffin. Anne White with her puffy white hair. Anne White who never bought our Girl Scout cookies and never let us play in her pool.

Jessica and I just stand there and stare at dead Anne White with her white pancake makeup in this room with windows that smells of dimestore perfume.

It's quiet in here. Just me and Jessica and white Anne White in her wooden coffin right in front of us.

Pretty soon we hear the lunch bell ring from across the street and we don't look both ways when we cross and we go back to Addison Elementary and we don't talk about Anne White or the way she won't be yelling at us from her window anymore.

After school, I walk home alone. I find three crates in the back yard, find John's handsaw and hammer and find seven nails in the garage and I make a little wooden coffin, just my size.

I drag the thing around to the side of the house where there isn't a walkway and I tuck my coffin in between the wooden fence and the big avocado tree. I know it's an avocado tree because John says it's an avocado tree, but the avocados are hard and small and you can't eat them. Anyway. I climb into my coffin and I lay perfectly still. I rest my hands on my heart. My coffin.

"Ariel?"

I can hear my mother calling me.

"Ariel?"

I pretend not to hear.

"Ariel?"

Now I can hear John calling me, too.

Louder. "Ariel?"

But my coffin used to be a tree and my coffin whispers in my ear. My coffin tells me it's OK if people can't find you sometimes.

If they find me, I'll say I was asleep.

But they don't find me. Pretty soon they stop calling my name.

landslide

Yesterday was exciting because Addison Elementary School was one of the polling places. People came to vote in our library. But this morning is not exciting. My mother says this morning is a dark day in America. We have lost. Ronald Reagan has won the presidency by a landslide. That means he got a lot of votes. It is not the same as a mudslide that comes after a long draught. Leslie says the vote was rigged, but John says it's worse than that: All those people actually voted for Ronald Reagan. And now he's going to be the president and every single one of us is going to die. Reagan wants to blow up the whole world. I don't know why he wants to do it. He'll die, too, unless he escapes in a rocket ship to outer space. And he can do it. There's a button in an office somewhere and he can just push it and that will send a nuclear bomb to Russia and then the Russians will see it coming and a nuclear bomb will come here and Russia and America are both really big and the whole world will blow up.

Last month, me and Minnie Wong went door to door selling oatmeal cookies and collecting money for Jimmy Carter's campaign. We raised $71, but then we got tired of ringing doorbells and we took some of the money and we bought mint chip ice cream cones at Swensen's and we only sent $67.50 to the campaign and now we are going to die in the nuclear holocaust.

5 o'clocks

At 5 o'clock in Carmel, Grandma takes a gin and tonic. Grandpa takes a vodka tonic. Grandma gives me tonic plain and I sneak a little bit of Gin and Vodka in it. We call the drinks 5 o'clocks. Most days, if I haven't seen my dad by the time Grandpa pours our 5 o'clocks, I can expect to see him for dinner. But it's a cool August night after I've turned eleven—five minutes past 5 o'clock—and Grandpa points the remote control at the TV and turns off the nightly news. He swings his armchair around so that he faces the middle of the living room. Grandma sets down her gin and tonic on a little yellow coaster. I'm holding my left foot up behind my butt and hoping around the glass coffee table when she makes the announcement: "Your father won't be coming today," she says gravely. "He isn't well."

I stop hopping and stand still on my one leg, facing Grandma. I wish Leslie had come to Carmel with me this time. She would have known just what to say and even if she didn't it would have been her saying it. I just stand there on one leg. It was the first time I'd ever heard anyone in Carmel say anything about my dad's health.

"You don't think we'll catch it, do you?" I ask.

Grandma takes a sip of her drink and sets it down. "Certainly not if he doesn't come to dinner."

"But he came to dinner last time," I remind her.

Grandma folds her hands in her lap. "He wasn't ill last time."

"Sure he was," I say as I start hoping around the coffee table again. "He's had schizophrenia for ten years, maybe more!"

Grandma doesn't say anything.

Grandpa sips his vodka tonic.

The quiet makes my stomach feel tingly, so I pick up my pace. The coffee table is wedged too close to the couch, which makes that part of my hopping journey especially difficult. It occurs to me that I shouldn't have singled my dad out as having schizophrenia. Grandma had been the one to bring it up, but I knew it made her sad to think about it. I want to change the subject. My mother once told me that the reason mental illness makes people feel so sad is that they imagine they're all alone, like they're the only ones who have it. I try to think of other people who have schizophrenia. Maybe I can tell Grandma about them, and then she won't feel so sad. But I can't think of anybody. I stop hopping. The only sound I can hear is the muffled crashing of waves on the beach outside. "Don't be sad, Grandma!" I finally blurt. "Gammie Evelyn has alcoholism and Uncle Dan is a homo." I plop myself down on the carpet. At least if Grandma doesn't feel less alone, she'll smile. Grown-ups always smile when a kid says "homo." But as soon as I look up, I know: In Carmel, grown-ups do not smile when a kid said "homo."

My grandparents sit motionless on opposite sides of the living room. I take my glass of tonic from the coffee table and finished it off in one gulp. "Lots of people have schizophrenia, too," I try.

Grandpa swings his chair around and turns the nightly news back on.

Grandma stares at me, clears her throat. "Your father," she says, enunciating carefully. "Has a cold." And then she stands up, gin and tonic in hand, and she marches into the kitchen.

I start to stand, but something inside of me pops open. Like when you yawn after a plane ride and your ears pop open. Like that, only not just my ears. There's a clicking noise, but no warning. I realize that the sound I've taken for waves crashing on the beach outside hasn't been waves at all but a chorus of whispers, soft voices hissing from every corner of the yellow living room. *Disappeared.* The voices swirled around me until one voice rises up above all the others and hisses, "Get her."

Before I can whisper "who?" My legs stand up underneath me and carry me into the kitchen faster than I knew I could sprint. "Grandma!" I'm not thinking. It's a scary feeling, not knowing myself what I'm going to say or do. It occurs to me, fleetingly, that I'm almost as big as my grandmother, and certainly stronger. If the whisperers say to take her, I could take her. But instead I open my mouth: "Nobody gives a shit about the golf course doily. We want Crab Louis!" I scream. "And you aren't innocent. None of you."

When my grandmother looks up from her dishes, her stare isn't blank. She looks genuinely sad. The whisperers are silent. I turn around slowly, run. If Grandpa looks over from his TV-watching or swings his armchair around to face me, I don't see him do it. I run down my grandparent's soft hall, into the back bedroom, and I hide under the yellow comforter. I stay there, perfectly still, for a long time. I can't tell if I'm falling asleep or waking. I feel puffed up, lighter than I've ever felt—and bigger. The physical laws that dictate the boundary between me and not-me are suspended. *Was this what it always felt like just before I fell asleep?* Maybe I just hadn't noticed before. I listen hard for the whisperers. I suspect they have the answers. But all I can hear is the muffled sound of the waves crashing on the beach outside.

August 8, 1981

Dear Ariel,

We have decided that it is best for you and it is best for us if we let the years slip by without any visits. The nice times you had here in Carmel were all a part of your childhood. The years go by fast and before you know it you will be a mature young lady. There can always be good that comes from seemingly sad situations and I hope on the good side of recent events is a lesson you can learn. It is the lesson that once something is said it can never be unsaid, much as we might wish it so.

Love,
Grandma

August 10, 1981

Dear Ariel,

你好吗

Well, you seem to have caused quite a disturbance when you were down here at mother's, even though I understand you were sick with a cold. Bernard Shaw, who could write in the newspapers, tried a good deal to do something about the problems in Ireland by writing about them, and James Joyce never went back to Ireland for twenty-seven years.

It's been foggy around Carmel. It doesn't feel like summer at all. A tiger looks like this:

虎

The old Chinese character

for a tiger's stripes changed to

虍

this over the years and adding the hind legs

儿

the character for tiger looks like this:

虎

Mao the Cat is still searching for a way out. Here is a picture of a medfly:

Aug 10
← MEDFLY

See you soon.

*Love,
Dad*

But I did not see my dad soon. We let the years slip by. Because that's the kind of people we are.

Part Two:
Love in the '80s
Or:
"Hitchhiking to the Mental Hospital"

william the pig

The Lehman's had this pig in their back yard. A pet pig named William the pig.

I wasn't really friends with those Lehman kids. They had sandy-colored hair and buttons for noses. My mom was friends with their mom, with Libby Lehman. They were in poetry group together. "There's a darkness to Libby's poetry," my mother said, but I was just straight-up jealous of those Lehman kids 'cause they had this big pinkish-greyish-black William in their back yard, and that pig was so cute and a little bit hairy—you know, sort of peach-fuzzy like pigs are.

"I wish I had a pig," I sighed to the older Lehman girl. She was my sister's age, maybe, tall and pretty.

She didn't answer me. She just shook her head and shrugged, like *whatever*.

But then one day we went over and Mr. Lehman wouldn't let me go in the back yard to see William—he just tugged at his beard and shook his head. And Libby Lehman set the long dining room table with the good silver and she served us pork chops for dinner, with dark sweet barbeque sauce. And I played Tinker Toys in the shag-carpeted den with those Lehman kids.

It was maybe a year after that when the phone rang at our house too early and it was one of those Lehman kids, voice shaky and too high-pitched so I handed the phone over to my stepdad.

Mr. Lehman, it turned out, had accidentally shot Libby Lehman in the chest while he was cleaning his gun that morning and no, they hadn't called 911 yet, they needed a priest, not a paramedic.

That seemed like a strange story, but my stepdad the priest put on his wool beret and my mom the poet put on her coral red lipstick and the back door to our house slammed behind them and Libby Lehman was dead.

When my parents got home, my stepdad said, "I don't think that was an accident."

And my mother sighed and shook her head and said, "*Of course* that wasn't an accident."

But the newspaper said it was an accident and Mr. Lehman kept going to work every day and the Lehman kids kept going to school every day and I thought about William the pig and the way that before Mr. Lehman killed Libby, he must have killed William the Pig.

does it hurt?

In Mr. Heineken's fourth grade class, Jessica sat behind me. She gave me the things she didn't like from her lunch box—Fritos and strawberry fruit rolls—exotic things they didn't sell at the co-op, things that had preservatives in them.

At music time we sang Johnny Cash songs and show tunes and *I'm just an elevator op-erator, you look to me like a hot to-ma-toe.*

At recess, Jessica kissed the boy we called "Brice-a-Roni."

But now we are not in fourth grade anymore. Now we are not singing and kissing. Now Jessica is at Stanford Hospital because she has bone cancer.

I meet Minnie Wong at Woolworth's and we steal fake ruby birthstone earrings and we take the bus to Stanford Hospital and we find the white room.

Jessica looks small in her bed, she smiles shy freckles. She pulls back the white sheet to show us the damage. "Like my leg?" she wants to know, but it isn't her whole leg, it's just her thigh and a dark red scar-wound that snakes across the end of it.

"We brought you earrings," I try, and show her the fake rubies.

Minnie Wong stares at the scar-wound for a long time. "Does it hurt?" she wants to know. "Where they cut it?"

Jessica shakes her head, points further down. "It hurts there," she says. "Where my leg used to be."

beachcomber

Leslie and my mom have a new doctor named Rosa Pomodoro. She is not the kind of doctor they have at Stanford Hospital. Dr. Pomodoro is a past-life regression therapist. Leslie was an Egyptian queen in her past life—not Cleopatra, but an important one. A forgotten Egyptian queen. In my mom's past life, she was an operative in the Mexican revolution. She was involved in a complicated and politically-significant love triangle. In their most recent past lives, both Leslie and my mom died in concentration camps in Germany. Just like Anne Frank. This is why we can't eat German food.

I want to find out who I was in my past life, but I'm afraid it won't be anything important, and then Leslie and my mom will know that's why I'm not as smart as they are. I'm afraid Dr. Pomodoro will tell me that I was a sad housewife in Cupertino. Or a beachcomber.

My dad is a beachcomber. He got a metal detector and he drags it all over Carmel Beach. When the detector beeps. he digs up pennies and scrap metal. He writes me postcards, telling me about it. One day he's going to find something that's worth a lot of money, like a diamond ring or a bar of gold. When he finds the treasure, he's going to sell it and send me some of the money.

If I was a beachcomber in my past life, I hope I was one who found a treasure.

aliens

"There are seven African powers," Leslie says. And she's bringing them all down in our back yard. She's got a book about the seven African powers. "These powers—they all represent different archetypes. Different *kinds* of power and magic."

I nod as she explains, squinting my eyes and trying to look enlightened.

"I have to wait until Mom and John aren't here to bring down the powers," she says, "but I know they're going out on Saturday. Dr. Pomodoro is giving a lecture at the community center." She bites her thumbnail. "I kind of want to go to the lecture. But these powers. They're asking to come down."

On Saturday afternoon my mom and John head out to the lecture and Leslie collects candles and herbs and colored pieces of cloth from around the house for her ritual.

I sneak out the side door and find my old crate coffin wedged in between the fence and avocado tree. I lay down in it, but I have to bend my knees a little to fit now. I close my eyes, hear Leslie chanting until I don't hear her anymore.

I wake suddenly to a shrill voice and the smell of smoke. It's our new neighbor who lives in Anne White's old house and she's screaming "I've called the fire brigade!" The sirens in the distance sing their siren song and then closer and Leslie running around the side of the house yelling, "Oh my God," and crackling sounds and I lift myself up out of my coffin and I creep around to the back yard, and I watch as two firemen put the out the small blaze with their hoses while Leslie talks to a third fireman and he writes things down. When the firemen leave, Leslie just stands there, her gaze fixed on the side stucco wall of the garage, at a smoke-black image of a skull that has burned itself there. She turns around slowly to face me. "Don't tell Mom and John," is all she says. And she takes off running.

I figure my mom and John will find out soon enough about the African powers and the skull and the fire brigade, but I sure won't be the one to tell them. I'm sitting in the kitchen when they get home. My mom looks depressed, her lipstick faded, and John seems anxious, so I wonder if they already know, but it turns out they're upset about the lecture.

"I need some chamomile tea," my mother says gravely as she sets the water to boil.

I want Swiss Miss.

"It was a talk about alien abductions," John explains, clasping his hands in front of him.

"And *everyone* there had been abducted," my mom says. "We felt so left out. What's wrong with us? Why wouldn't aliens want to abduct *us*?"

John nods. "Dr. Pomodoro says that alien abductions are actually quite common, but I'm still a bit skeptical."

"Did it sound like fun?" I try. "Getting abducted?" But my mom and John ignore me.

"How on earth can you be skeptical?" My mom is asking John. She pours hot water for her tea. "Do you think all of those people are *crazy*? They all had the same story. Do you think they've had a *collective hallucination*?"

John shrugs as he leaves us in the kitchen. "I'm not sure," he says. "I'm just saying I'm skeptical. There's just very little scientific evidence."

I rip open my Swiss Miss packet and pour the chocolate powder into the bottom of my mug. My mother pours the water for me and I stir, but before I even get a chance to take a sip, John comes rushing back in. "What's that in the back yard?"

My mother and I follow John down the hall and out the back door. He points to the burned image of the skull.

I just stare.

My mother places her hand over her heart. "Could it be?" she gasps. "Could it be the aliens?"

I'm thinking about my Swiss Miss.

aunt rose

My Aunt Rose wants to know if I take skim milk, lowfat milk, or whole milk in my cereal. "What do you take, Ariel?"

I don't know what I take. *What do I take?* Skim, I decide. "I take skim."

I don't really know my Aunt Rose. She never sends a birthday card. But for some reason she has invited me to her home for the weekend and for some reason I have been delivered here.

"Skim? Are you on a diet, dear? I'm so glad. I wasn't going to say anything but I think that's smart. A woman can never be too rich or too thin, as they say." My Aunt Rose sort of snickers when she says this and I don't know why she's snickering. If she's kidding or if she's laughing at me or what.

Skim.

I didn't know that skim meant diet. I decide that "skim" must be related to "slim" which I know is related to "thin" which I now know I can never be "too" of.

"Are you learning enough about calories?" My Aunt Rose wants to know. "Because if you're going to be on a diet you'll have to count your calories. That means no mayonnaise and no butter. And when you learn about calories it can be confusing. A serving of carrots might have thirty calories, say, but that doesn't mean that one carrot has thirty calories. You have to find out how many carrots there are in the *serving* and how big the carrots are."

Everything seems complicated.

I pour the grayish milk onto my raisin bran. I wish I'd said I took some other kind of milk. The raisins are sweet and they puff a little in the milk but the milk tastes like it's half water.

My Aunt Rose blabs on: "One of the gals I play tennis with went on a diet because her husband was going to leave her. Or so she thought. She decided to lose twenty pounds and you know what? She did it. She lost those twenty pounds. She could have fit into her wedding dress, I tell you. And I'll be darned, they're still married. You can't argue with that."

I guess you can't.

Argue with that.

big red

My Gammie Evelyn drives a big red Cadillac. She calls it Big Red and it smells like Coco Chanel.

We speed all over Orange County because Big Red can handle the speed bumps and the police never stop my Gammie when she's driving Big Red. It's summertime, of course. It's always summertime in Orange County because I'm on break from school and the sun is shining. It might be summer break or Thanksgiving break or winter break or spring break. It doesn't matter. It's summertime when she picks me up at John Wayne Airport and my Gammie says, "You're beautiful, Ariel, but you've got to be kidding with that hair. Can't you put it up? I mean, honestly."

"You're marvelous of course," she says. "Do you have a beau?"

"No," I tell my Gammie. I don't have a beau.

And she says, "Well, not now, but soon the fellows will want to take you out and just remember, you don't pay. When a fellow takes you out, he pays the bill."

I'm 12 years old and I listen intently because my Gammie is beautiful and she wears red lipstick and she paints her long fingernails red and she wears her hair in a bun tied with a bright red scarf as she speeds down the Pacific Coast Highway in Big Red.

My Gammie Evelyn's house is painted coral orange.

Inside, there's soft, plush coral carpet, and in the guest bedroom soft, plush yellow monogrammed towels.

How are her towels always so soft?

On the low black coffee table in the living room there's a big crystal bowl full of mint and chocolate candy.

How is the candy never stale?

I sit on the plush carpet in front of the coffee table and I eat and I eat and I wonder how my Gammie Evelyn keeps that bowl full, how she keeps herself from eating it all when she gets up in the middle of the night to pour herself a glass of milk and bourbon.

love

I am in love with Reina Mendoza's big sister.

My sister, Leslie, says that you can tell you're in love with someone if you can't live without them. She says that's the *definition* of love. She says I can't understand anything about love seeing as I'm only twelve, but I know that I cannot live without Reina Mendoza's big sister.

Her name is Gloria. She has big beautiful almond eyes and heart-shaped lips and everyone says she looks just like Irene Cara but I swear she's prettier.

Gloria says that people like us with hair like ours—she calls it *kinky*—she says we're special. She says it's the '80s now and everyone wants to look like us and those little white girls with their straight white-girl hair—they're totally *over*. She says I look like Jennifer Beals from *Flashdance*.

Gloria is only seventeen, but she has a little boy named Lionel. She named him after Lionel Richie.

When I take the bus to her apartment and we go to Menalto Market, I pretend that Lionel is *my* baby and I hold him on my hip. We walk through the aisles and I look at the individually-wrapped orange cheese slices and I look at the chicken-flavored Top Ramen and I look at the six-packs of Dr. Pepper and I pretend that I'm shopping for my family. Then Gloria pretends that me and Lionel are both her kids—she thinks I look that much like her—and, yeah, she had us young, but if I'm her kid she must be at least 21, right? So we can get the beer, right?

"Of course, baby," the guy behind the register says.

Guys always call Gloria "baby." And they always give her anything she wants. I'm telling you, she's that pretty.

Sometimes the kids outside Menalto Market call me a honkey, but Gloria says I'm not a honkey because I'm Italian.

She's going to be a model, Gloria is. And she says I can be a model, too. She says it doesn't matter if we're not five-foot-eleven because it's the '80s now and we're exotic. When we become models we're going to get an apartment in New York City and we'll take turns taking care of Lionel and we'll have a fire escape instead of a porch and we'll sit out there in the purple sunset and we will be the pretty people.

We will be the pretty people.

possessed

I'm standing in the bathroom with Leslie, watching in the mirror as she applies layer after layer of white pancake makeup. "Do you see how one of my eyes goes a little to the right?" she asks. I do not see this when she looks at me, but when we look together at her reflection in the mirror, I see what she means.

"People used to get burned at the stake for having a go-funny eye," she says. "People used to think it meant you were crazy. But it really just means that you have one eye on the other world."

I nod.

"Have you ever been possessed?" Leslie wants to know.

"I don't think so."

"Dr. Pomodoro says I'm possessed." Leslie exhales real slow. "It's not like the Exorcist or anything. You just get a spirit with you and if it's a good spirit you feel present and connected—that's more like an angel—but usually the spirits who attach themselves to living people have unfinished business here. They got stuck here. So they make you angry or depressed or mean or just feel really heavy. They try to finish their business through you."

"I hope I never get possessed," I say.

And Leslie nods. "Yeah, the spirits are sort of a pain in the ass. But if you keep an eye out, you can see them coming."

threadbare

Seventh grade starts out well enough: Three new outfits from Contempo Casuals, a fake Izod shirt, and a pair of Jordache Jeans.

Jessica and I have all the same classes together. She's good in Spanish. Our biology teacher makes us pledge allegiance to the flag. After school we head over to Jessica's two-storied house and we listen to Blondie. Or we go to Swensen's Ice Cream on University Avenue and sit up on the balcony and drop ice cubes onto the teenage punk rocker's bald heads as they scurry along the sidewalk below.

We wear frosted blue eye shadow to the fall dance.

I spend the night at her house and we watch her parent's dirty movies on the VCR in the back cottage.

But by the middle of the year it's all getting shaky, disintegrating into the same four boring outfits, threadbare from the washer dryer washer dryer and not even enough of them to get through the week without a repeat outfit. Then the drama of the heavy metal chicks and the back-stabbing bitches and December-January— Jessica has to have a biopsy. *What's a biopsy?* Nothing much, just a test, they have to check on something, do minor surgery, see if the cancer's back. Probably it won't be back. Probably it's nothing. I eat a cheeseburger in the Stanford Hospital cafeteria with Jessica's dad and we talk about nothing. He looks like Robert Redford.

By Spring break, everything's all right again. *Don't worry about it.* Jessica spends the night at my house and we stay up late planning a party for the end of June—a week after my birthday, a week before her's. She tries to convince me that her mom invented PAM, the no-stick cooking spray, but I think she's lying. She tells me that her mom used to be a world-class skier, but she hurt her knee. I say she's lying about that, too, but she's not. She calls her mom and her mom tells me herself about being a skier. But she doesn't say anything about the no-stick spray.

In the morning, the sun slants in through a gap in my flowered curtains. I poke Jessica's shoulder to wake her. At the foot of my double bed, two oval Easter baskets draped in fresh wisteria. Hand-blown eggs, chocolate eggs, flowers. Cool seventh-graders we're supposed to be, but we're crying.

That night we're on a Greyhound Bus—a Palo Alto City Parks and Rec. trip to Disneyland.

We pass neon-lit towns and Jessica throws up in the tiny bathroom. Two chaperones stand in the doorway, whispering.

I just sit there in the back of the bus, holding Jessica's prosthetic leg. I feel bad for her because she's sick. Maybe we just ate too much at the roadside stop. I feel bad for her because they won't let her puke in private, but I feel mad at her, too.

Jessica always finds a way to get all the attention.

After Spring break, Jessica doesn't come back to school. We talk on the phone and we try to visualize little Ms. Pac Mans gobbling up all the cancer cells.

We go to "Touchstone" meetings to talk about what it's like to be a kid with cancer, but it's a little weird, because I don't have cancer.

At school, the other seventh graders want to know when she's coming back, but I just shrug. "Soon."

She calls me one night in early June to say we won't be having that party together after all. She's going to Hawaii, she says. "I'm trying to stay focused on a picture of me healthy," she says, "but sometimes I just get a picture of myself cold and grey in a coffin."

I say, "don't worry, you're gonna get better really soon." But when I hang up, all I can see is Jessica cold and grey in that coffin.

I go outside, look for my old coffin between the fence and the avocado tree, but it's dark out and my coffin is gone.

bacardi & tab

There's a memorial at the Quaker Friends Meeting House. Lots of people talk about Jessica, but mostly I don't hear them. After the service, I ride my bike over to Reina and Gloria's apartment on Alma Street. All their stuff is in boxes. Reina keeps moving clothes and tapes and stuffed animals from one box to another and back again. Their mom got a job with Unicef, so they're moving. To Africa. To Botswana. All of them—even little Lionel. "You look sad," Gloria says.

"I am sad," I say. "Jessica died."

"Well," Gloria pouts, "me and Reina love you."

I shrug. "You and Reina are leaving."

Gloria hugs me, steps back, looks me up and down, says, "You know what, Girl? You need a drink. She grabs her LeSportsac purse and when she comes back she's got a bottle of Bacardi and a bottle of Tab and she sets the two bottles on a box and says, "Lionel's asleep on the mattress in my room. I'm going out."

Reina mixes our drinks in jars and we gulp them fast and we listen to the Southern Pacific trains passing and we smoke clove cigarettes that taste sweet on our lips and hot on our throats and we say mean things to each other and we cry and say "sorry" and we listen to Marvin Gaye and we throw up in the bathroom and we pass out next to Lionel on the mattress in Gloria's room and I wonder if this is what it feels like to be one of the pretty people.

accessory

The thing is, my stepdad is kind of dense. You'd think after all those years of being a priest and listening to all those confessions he wouldn't be so dense, but maybe some people are just dense. Anyway, my stepdad gives me the message from my sister like it's not even weird. He says, "Leslie called and she wants you to meet her at Stanford Shopping Center and bring big bags."

So I go into Leslie's room and I go under her bed and I get the bags. The Banana Republic bag and the Macy's bag and a couple of Contempo Casuals bags and the Victoria's Secret bag—plastic bags and big square paper bags with twine handles. I carry the empty bags out to the bus stop on Waverly and when the bus comes I climb on. I sit in the back with all the black kids who still sit in the back even though it's 1983 and their fathers are all doctors at Stanford Hospital.

At the mall, in front of The Gap, I meet Leslie and her friend Celine.

Leslie and Celine are supposed to be punks, but they're dressed like goth virgins in their short skirts and lacy tights, tank tops and bangles, white pancake make-up and kohl eyeliner, hair teased half way to San Jose.

When I show them the bags, Leslie says "thanks."

"Yeah, thanks," Celine says.

"Can I shop with you guys?" I ask, twirling a lock of hair around my finger, trying to act like I don't care.

They shrug and I follow them.

When they go into a shop, they each take one empty bag and by the time they come out, it's full. I wait outside. I sit on low cement walls, holding empty bags. They go into Victoria's Secret. They go in to The Gap. They go in to Contempo Casuals. I think maybe they're going to get me some lacy tights.

"We need more lingerie," Celine says.

Leslie nods. "We most definitely need more lingerie."

So they go into Macy's.

I sit on the wall, just a few empty bags in hand now.

A man sits next to me, glances up, says something into his Walkie Talkie. I think he's kind of creepy, the man. I wonder who he's talking to, if anyone. Maybe he's just pretending to talk on that Walkie Talkie. My mom says a grown woman was kidnapped from Stanford Shopping Center once. A grown woman. There was this man dressed up like an old lady and he got this woman's attention by acting confused, like a confused old lady, like he needed help, but he wasn't an old lady, he was a man and he was hiding an axe in his skirt. That's what I'm thinking about when Leslie and Celine come skipping out of Macy's with another full bag, and that's what I'm thinking about when another man with another Walkie Talkie appears from around a corner and the two of them are in front of Leslie and Celine and *Come with us* and *What? No, we didn't steal anything. We had this stuff from before.* And *young lady* and *security office* and I just sit there on the wall and watch as they all walk away.

I take the bus home.

I sit at the back next to Debbie Jones, who pretends she doesn't know me even though we're the only ones on the bus.

That night we're at the dining room table in the old Spanish house eating little Cornish game hens stuffed with bread and celery. Me and my mom and John. There's a place set for Leslie but she isn't there.

"Do you like the Cornish game hen?" my mother asks.

"They're my favorite," I lie.

And that's when there's a knock at the front door.

And that's when John answers it.

And that's when the cop who's got Leslie and Celine says, "Oh, Father Duryea? Is this *your* daughter?"

And that's when John looks at Leslie and says, "yes?" and tilts his head to the side.

And that's when my mom starts crying.

Later, Leslie and Celine will go to court and get convicted of grand theft. But the judge will know Father Duryea from the confessional, too, and Leslie and Celine won't have to go to juvie. They'll each be sentenced to 100 hours of community service, and they'll end up answering calls about suspicious warts on the V.D. hotline.

Me, I guess since I brought all those empty bags to Stanford Shopping Center I'm an accessory to grand theft, but no one ever says anything about that.

gabs

After Reina and Gloria's mom gets the job with Unicef and they all move to Botswana I don't hear from them.
So, that's it.
I don't hear from them.
You have friends and then you don't.
I don't hear from them for three months.
People leave. Simple. Traveling people, especially. They leave.
I don't hear from them for six months.

And then it arrives, the thin blue airmail envelope with the thinnest blue paper inside. And: *Hey, girl, why don't you come and visit us?*

Reina and Gloria want me to come and visit them. They want me to come all the way to Botswana.

I call a travel agent I know from John's church, but she says it'll cost me more than $1,000 to get to Botswana and back home again. I ask John if he has $1,000 and he laughs loud. He works at Printer's Ink Bookstore now and he says between his salary from church and his wages from the bookstore, it takes him a whole month to earn $1,000 and he has to spend that on the house and food.

So I start babysitting.

I babysit after school and I babysit in the evenings and I babysit on the weekends.

I babysit a little boy who lives in a big house with soft white carpet. He has seizures sometimes.

I babysit a first-grader on the south side of town. When the boy's father goes away on business, his stepmom goes out with a different man every night and whispers "please don't tell" and pays me extra. I sit on a big white bean bag chair and watch TV all night.

I babysit for a young couple whose infant baby is sleeping when I meet them and they give me all the instructions and then they leave and I sit on the frayed green couch in their living room, reading through a book of baby names. *Mabel, Mac, Maceo, Mackenzie, Macy.* When I finally go into the baby's room to check on him, his breath sounds wheezy and labored. *Maddox, Madison, Madonna, Mae, Maegan.* I'm startled when I see him. I just stand there, staring into the little doll-sized bassinet where he sleeps. He's the tiniest baby I've ever seen. *Is it really a baby?* He's hooked up to an IV. I could almost fit his whole body into one hand. *Maggie, Maia, Makalo, Malachi, Malcolm.* I stand there for a long time. Finally exhale, shrug off my shock. He's small, but he's still a baby. *He's a miniature baby*, I tell myself. I scoop him up, careful not to jiggle the IV.

When his parents finally get home, they smell like garlic and vodka. They giggle and blush and say, "We're sorry. Didn't we tell you he was premature?"

I babysit all autumn and I babysit all winter and I babysit into the spring and finally I save enough money and I buy my ticket to Botswana.

Botswana is a long way away.

Through Minneapolis and through London and through Johannesburg and onto a tiny plane like I'm Indiana Jones.

Gloria picks me up at the little one-room shack of an airport in Gaberone. She says they call it "Gabs."

In Gabs, we drive past houses made of tin and cardboard. The kids who play outside look like the African kids I've seen in *National Geographic* and they don't look like them at all. I can see the still images in their play. I can see the quick moments when I could click to create the same photo images. But the kids are real and they're here and they don't seem strange like the ones in the magazines. We jump rope.

In Gabs, the days stretch long.
I dream of water and blue sky.
Gloria says I should move here.
"You could be a Mendoza," she says.
I could be Ariel Mendoza.
I whisper my new name at night, whisper myself to sleep: *Ariel Mendoza.*
I dream of Palo Alto city buses and Southern Pacific trains.
Gloria says that when I move to Botswana, I can babysit Lionel.
Reina says that when I move to Botswana, we can share a room, the two of us. We can go to school together and I can wear the dark blue V-neck sweater and white shirt uniform like she does.
Reina and Gloria say that when I move to Botswana, my boyfriend will be Ben. He's the Nigerian diplomat's son.
Ben is fine, they say. Ben only listens to Michael Jackson. He wears white pants with lots of zippers on them.
When I move to Botswana, they say, Ben and I will dance every Saturday night at Club X.
But I don't live here yet.
So Gloria teases my hair tall and we all go to Club X and we drink pale beer and we dance to Sheila E.
I dance with Ben and he moonwalks under the mirrored disco ball. The strobe lights flash and flicker and Gloria whispers, "everyone's looking at you." And I'm not sure if I believe her.

They start playing *Dancing Queen...Only seventeen* and I'm dancing. I can feel it. I can feel they're looking at me. I *am* the queen.

The next week Reina's school lets out for break, so her mom says she's taking us all on a safari.

It's for real—I'm in Africa—I'm on safari in Africa—I'm in the Kalahari Desert where the Bushmen live. I'm a photographer. I take pictures of the elephants and I take pictures of the lions and I take pictures of the sapphire sunsets and I take pictures of the baobab trees and I take pictures of Gloria and little Lionel.

In a metal boat we *put-put* through the swamps, careful to avoid the alligators, and the African sun tinges my skin brown.

We sleep in dark tents, scared of the hippos grazing outside, scared of their silhouettes in the moonlight.

Gloria says, "You'll pass for colored now, Ariel, with your tan."

I'm excited to pass for colored, excited to know what that means, excited to go back to Gabs and dance at Club X and *pass*.

But when we get back to the city, Club X has been raided by the South African police.

And in the newspaper it says Club X was part of an arms-smuggling operation.

And in the newspaper it says the son of the Nigerian diplomat is dead.

And in the newspaper it says a lot of kids are dead.

Reina and Gloria's mom burns the muffins she's making and she throws them against the wall and she cries and she says we don't appreciate her and all that she does for us.

Reina and Gloria don't say anything about their mom or about the muffins or about Ben or about the dead kids at Club X, but it seems like maybe I'm not moving here.

It seems like maybe I'm going home soon.

bunny cho

"You were Jessica's friend," Bunny Cho says, pointing her chin at me. She's standing in front of City Lights Bookstore in San Francisco, wearing pin-striped pegged jeans and a black beret, her long black hair tucked behind her ears. "Right?" she says. "We go to middle school together? You were Jessica's friend?"

I never know what to say to that. *You were Jessica's friend.* It's not like I want to deny it, but I feel like such a fraud. I mean, *was I Jessica's friend?* When she called to say goodbye I told her she'd get better real soon. I lied to her when she was trying not to lie to me.

I shrug. "Yeah," I say. "I was her friend."

Bunny nods. She has a box of Nat Sherman Fantasia cocktail cigarettes and an old-fashioned flint lighter. "Well," she says. "That was sad. Smoke?"

Bunny lights a red cigarette from the box, puckers her lips around the gold filter, inhales, coughs just the slightest bit.

She hands me the turquoise cigarette and I think, *I'm going to be a real beatnik.* Gold and turquoise. The cigarette matches my turquoise Esprit Outlet T-shirt and gold leggings.

I AM San Francisco, I think.

But Bunny rolls her eyes at me. "Matches your winner-chick outfit," she says.

I pretend not to hear her. Being a "winner-chick," I know, is so much worse than being a loser. I inhale the tiniest puff of my turquoise cigarette—I don't want to give myself away. I puff out the smoke right away as Bunny blows rings into the night.

"What brand do you usually smoke?" Bunny wants to know.

I shrug. "Nat Sherman, too, of course. I just, you know, I ran out."

I bring the cigarette to my lips again. The smoke smells like school bathrooms and absent fathers. The inhalation hot on my throat. So much makes sense all the sudden. Love and death and the way God doesn't seem to give a shit. And I know I never want to breathe plain air again.

eighth grade

I listen to Prince. *1999*. I calculate my age. I'll be 29 in the year 2000—*no way!*—I'll never be that old.

I start eighth grade. I leave seventh grade things behind. I wear hats like Bunny Cho. I am a punk rocker and I wear ripped jeans. I am a mod and I wear little vintage dresses. "You have to decide," my sister says. "Mod or rocker? Prince is out. *Quadrophenia* is everything."

I learn to throw up.

I eat and throw up and smoke cigarettes to soothe my throat.

I weigh 125 pounds. I weigh 120 pounds. I weigh 110 pounds. I weigh 98 pounds. I weigh 97 pounds. I weigh 95 pounds. My friends are going to the psych ward for losing a lot less weight than this, but I guess they've got health insurance better than Medi-Cal or something because no one suggests the psych ward for me. I want to go to the psych ward so bad. I want to throw fits when those bitches in the cafeteria try to put mayonnaise on my sandwich. I want to be studied. I want to be anorexic, but I don't have the willpower. I plateau at 95 pounds. I eat frozen yogurt. I dye my hair black. I dye my hair magenta. I dye my hair black again. I wear hats.

san quentin

My mom gets her master's degree and a new job to go with it: She teaches art to prisoners on death row at San Quentin.

She gets a T-shirt that says, "Why do we kill people who kill people to show people that killing people is wrong?"

She says, "I told the guys I had a daughter and they asked for naked pictures of you." She laughs. "I gave them picture of you naked when you were five. Isn't that funny?"

I don't think it is so funny, but I'm not sure I know what I think.

San Quentin is a fortress, a pale yellow castle on the bay. I go with my mom to the visiting room on the row to meet "the guys."

Parking lot, security check, metal detector, security check, door, walk, door, click, door, lights.

The guys don't look that tough, but I guess they are. Mass murderers, child killers, night stalkers, innocents waiting for the DNA tests that will never clear them.

One of the child killers stares at me too long and my mother nudges me and says "I can't believe you didn't wear a bra."

But I am. Wearing a bra.

One of the innocent guys says he's psychic. "I predict that you will go to Egypt one day," he tells me, and he clasps his hands on his lap. "There, you will find two golden ankhs. You must buy them."

I never go to Egypt, but I go to an art show a few of years later, "The Art of Death Row," and there I am in the paintings, my 14-year-old self looking innocent and not-very-psychic in the middle of a dartboard. My 14-year-old face as the face of a mare throwing her head back to reveal a vulnerable neck. The artist had been sentenced to death for slitting the throats of two 14-year-olds.

green gultch farm

"Are you a crazy person?" The driver leans across the passenger's seat to open the door of her bashed-up silver hatchback for me. "Nobody hitchhikes anymore." She's missing a couple of teeth and her car's a mess of crumpled papers and food wrappers. I already like her.

I climb in. "I'm going to Green Gulch. A few miles up—"

"The Zen Center?" She laughs as she accelerates. "Buckle in, kid." She turns up the volume on her car stereo. Gerry Garcia singing about driving some train. My ride lets me off at the top of the driveway. "Good luck and don't hitchhike," she says.

I make my way down into the gulch, along a marked path, and into a wooden office. I hand over my $25 and a robed woman with a shaved head leads me to my room. Just a bed and a window. "Vegetarian dinner is served at six," she says. "Zazen at five a.m."

I stash my little pack under the bed and creep outside, hike down past the farm and to the beach in the fading sunlight. I could stay here, I think. Just be a monk. Shave my head.

Back up in my little room, I lay down for a few minutes before dinner, but I fall asleep hard and dreamless and when I wake it's to the sound of a gong in the near distance, foggy dawn outside my little window.

I shuffle down the hallway to a small bathroom, wash my face in the sink, then follow the silent monks outside and along the narrow dirt path toward a wooden temple.

"Come in," a robed man at the door beckons. I sit on a round, black cushion. The sound of another gong. I face the wall. I listen tired. The robed man who led us all into the temple tells us that the Zen tradition of meditation comes to us in an Asian envelope, but it isn't Asian. "Zazen isn't Eastern or Western," he says. "Zazen just is. We sit. We do not close our eyes," he says. "We cannot close our ears or our noses, and so we do not close our eyes. Our gaze is lowered, but our eyes remain open."

I lower my gaze. I'm thinking about death and calories.

"Our posture is balanced, grounded, open," the man says. "Our legs are crossed in front of us. Our hands rest, palms up, left over right, just below the navel, thumbs touching and yet not touching."

I cup my hands, let my thumbs touch just slightly.

"From here there is nothing to do," the man says. "We simply sit. If thoughts arise we make no judgments. We let them arise. We let them go. If it helps to quiet the mind, we may choose to count our breaths. Counting each inhalation and each exhalation, we begin with one and we count to ten, then we begin again. At one."

There is the muffled sound of bodies shifting, but mostly there is no sound. Then the sound of the gong reverberating through the Zendo.

All quiet. We sit. Inhale. Exhale. I count my breaths. Thoughts arise. Cigarettes and miniature babies. Inhale. Exhale. I sit perfectly still. It has been a long time or it has not been so long.

Another gong, and everyone rises. I follow them, and they begin their walking mediation. I walk behind them. I bow when they bow. I sit again when they sit again. Inhale. Exhale. Thoughts arise. The shape of Gloria's mouth when she said I could be a Mendoza. And then it's all quiet. I count my breaths.

At breakfast, no one speaks. I fill my bowl with oatmeal and nectarine slices, pour soy milk from a pitcher. I take a seat at one of the long tables, look around at all the strangers. The robed man from mediation sits across from me and two chairs down. A skinny guy in sweats and a flowing hippie shirt sits next to me. A woman in loose jeans and a T-shirt and an older-looking woman with a shaved head sit at the end of our table. All silence.

Finally, another gong and a woman with a giant gray Afro laughs loud. "Good morning, Buddhas!" she cries out. "You can talk now."

And everyone starts talking and laughing. The skinny guy sitting next to me addresses the robed man from our mediation. "Roshi, I've been a vegetarian for fifteen years," he brags.

The Roshi smirks. "And that's gotten you pretty close to enlightenment?"

The skinny guy sort of nods and shakes his head at the same time.

There's a boyish gleam in the Roshi's eye. "What do you say you and I go into town for lunch and get ourselves a couple of hot dogs?"

The skinny guy looks at the Roshi wide-eyed. The other people at the table just watch.

But Roshi smiles open-hearted. "That's exactly what we need," he nods. "It's settled. We need a couple of hot dogs."

The old bald woman bursts open with her laughter now. "Hot dogs," she squeals. "We need hot dogs."

well of anger

"You have a well of anger," Leslie tells me. "And your inability to express your anger will be your demise."

She's just moved to the city and we're standing in the misty rain outside her apartment. Dark night in the Tenderloin. She's seventeen or eighteen, my sister. She just finished high school.

She knows a lot, my sister, and the things she seems to know about me scare me. "The Greeks say everyone has a fatal flaw," she says. "*Fatal*," her blue eyes narrow. "And this is yours—this anger you have. I can see it—it's almost an entity that surrounds you." She nods as she talks and she drags on her hand-rolled cigarette.

I light a Lucky Strike.

"I'm only telling you this so you can deal with it," she says. "You can't see it at all, can you?" She stares at me.

I stare back.

"You think that the way you are—you think it's sagely or something. But you're angry. You're repressed. You don't understand what I'm saying, do you? Maybe you're just too young to get it."

I want to understand what my sister is saying because she's smart and beautiful and she has a psychiatrist and a hypnotherapist and she has past lives in Paris and Bombay and Egypt and once a month she gets a migraine headache which means the spirits are coming down into her brain and taking possession. She's possessed, my sister. And I know I'll never be that deep.

An ambulance sirens by and I become aware of all the cars on Jones Street, the sounds, the space that's bigger than my sister and me. "Can we go inside?" I ask. "In your apartment?" I drop my half-smoked cigarette onto the sidewalk and crush it with my Doc Marten.

My sister studies my face. "You know," she finally says. "I'm going to say no. I can't let you into my home until you deal with this anger problem. It's just the energy around you. I can't. I need to protect my new space. I mean, I don't want to send you back to the Transbay Terminal all by yourself, but we'll get you a taxi to the Southern Pacific Station." My sister waves her hand absently toward the street until a yellow cab stops at the corner. "Do you have any money?" she asks as I duck into the back seat.

Later, when I'm smoking Nat Sherman Black & Gold cocktail cigarettes with Bunny Cho under the train bridge in Palo Alto, I try to explain to her about my well of anger. I try to explain about how it's going to be my demise, this anger, about how I'm not really sure how to deal with it. *My fatal flaw.*

"I mean, I think I need a psychiatrist or a hypnotherapist or something," I say.

Bunny laughs, pushes her fingers through her hair. "Anybody could say that about anybody." She purses her lips and pretends to be my sister: "*Oh, you have a well of anger.*" She shakes her head. "That's bullshit," she says. "Your sister is completely insane."

And I wonder if that's true, that anybody could say that about anybody.

the new varsity

I work at the New Varsity Theater downtown selling movie tickets and candy. All the punk rockers hang out in the patio. Rocky Horror at midnight. Second run movies at five and seven. Old Phil works the projection booth upstairs. He's union, I guess.

I get paid $3.65 an hour but sometimes I sell both ends of the tickets and pocket the extra cash.

"You can get in a lot of trouble for doing that," Phil tells me.

I figure he means I can get fired.

"Everybody does it," I tell him.

"Cops don't care what everybody does. They'll still bust you." Phil licks his yellow teeth. He's a methadone junkie, Phil. "Got hooked in 'nam," he says. He's always broke. "Give me some Good & Plenty?"

I grab a box of Good & Plenty and slide it across the glass counter.

Phil doesn't say "thank you," just: "Come up to the projection booth after the movie starts?"

Once the movie starts and everything gets quite in the lobby, I tip toe in through the theater and up the red-carpeted stairs to the projection booth, creak the door open, climb the black painted stairs to where Phil's sitting on a low chair. "What's up?"

"Why don't you come and sit on my lap," he whispers.

I don't really want to sit on Phil's lap, but I figure it beats having to talk to the cops about selling both ends of the tickets so I sit on his lap. I watch the movie through the little square window. It's *Witness*. Harrison Ford.

I can feel Phil hard against my butt.

Phil puts his hands on my hips and says, "Ariel, you know I'd never call the cops on you, don't you?"

I push myself up off his hard dick and his bony knees and I shrug. "Sure, Phil. I know." I creep out of the projection booth and I feel like such an idiot.

I'm never gonna tell anybody I sat on that junkie's lap.

bijou

I work at the Bijou Theater, too, on Emerson Street. I sell tickets and candy and sometimes I run the projector.

Behind the concessions counter the salty butter smell—everything sticky with Diet Coke syrup. Bunny is upstairs in the projection booth. I've been running back and forth between concessions and ticket sales. Sold-out Saturday matinee showing of *Kiss of the Spider Woman*. Our boss Faye was a no-show. Instead of Faye, we found a scribbled note from our other boss, Agnes.

"I can't fucking believe this," Bunny says when the rush is over, when the movie is finally onscreen and we're alone behind the concessions counter. She squints at the note. "The mental hospital? Why'd she have to go crazy? I mean, they were like *our parents*. Agnes and Faye. First they get divorced and now Faye has to go totally insane?"

I grab a handful of popcorn, nibble a kernel, think about that: *Our parents.*

Maybe there's something about me that makes parents go crazy.

Agnes and Faye, our theater managers.

But then Agnes had an affair with Litty, the concessions lady who brought all the Snickers bars and the boxes of Good & Plenty and soft-drink syrups down from San Francisco. And then Faye went crazy. And now we're orphans, me and Bunny and all the other kids who work at the theaters. Orphans, just like that.

"I guess we should go visit her," Bunny sighs. "In the fucking mental hospital."

And I guess she's right.

Our shift ends after the last matinee starts. We could steal some money out of the till, take the train down to San Jose, hitchhike from the station to the mental hospital.

"That's what we'll do," Bunny says. "Hitchhike to the mental hospital." She lights a cigarette.

We're not allowed to smoke behind the concessions counter—only in the projection booth or outside. But I guess it doesn't matter, seeing as our boss is in the mental hospital.

Bunny passes me a cigarette, and I light it.

cocaine hangover

I work at Ramona's Pizza, too. I serve beer even though I'm underage and I sneak pizzas out to the runaways in the alley.

Kelly is our manager. She says we should call her "mom" but she's nothing like my mom and nothing like Agnes or Faye and nothing like the mom I'd want. Kelly's in recovery. She says it all proud like we could never hope to be so accomplished: *Recovery.*

At the staff meeting she shakes her head at us and clenches her little fists. She says she knows we're all doing cocaine in the staff room on breaks and she doesn't appreciate it. She doesn't appreciate it one bit. But she's here for us. She's here for any one of us who wants to talk about the dangers of cocaine and the thrill of recovery. "Have I called in sick one day in the past year?" she asks. We all stare at her. It's a rhetorical question. We are fourteen and sixteen and eighteen. We are high school students and high school drop-outs. "No," she says, raising her little fist in the air. "I have not called in sick, and do you know why that is?"

I'm shaking my head, trying to look like I care.

"It's because I feel *great*," Kelly says. "Compared to the way I used to feel every day—with that cocaine hangover—I could have the worst flu now, a migraine, I could have a brain tumor the size of a grapefruit now and I would feel *great*."

I nod, trying to look moved, hoping she'll go home after the meeting so I can go in the break room and do a line.

pacheco pass

When I fell in love with Sabine, I still didn't understand why all the wrong people looked so pretty. I figured maybe it wasn't love, exactly. I figured maybe I just wanted to *be* her. Sabine.

Her hair was long and soft and wavy. Her eyes were dark with flecks of gold. She was French, Sabine. Her mother yelled at her on the phone in French and I thought that was so cool.

Sabine worked at the pizza parlor with me and all the waiters were in love with her even though she dressed fully 1969—handwoven Guatemalan shirts, a hundred bangles on her wrists, ripped jeans under Indian skirts, bright hair wraps on a dozen random locks of her long hair. Sabine. Total hippie circa 1986 in Palo Alto. But she could get away with it. She was that pretty.

All the waitresses called Sabine a slut, but I liked her. I would have followed her anywhere, Sabine.

Pretty. I guess that's how I found myself following Sabine as she followed the Grateful Dead in a paisley-painted 1969 VW van all the way down the West Coast and back again. We drove all night and we smoked pot in the morning. We drove all day and we pulled over to sleep.

Which is how I find myself now: Sleeping in that paisley-painted 1969 VW van in the parking lot of Casa de Fruta in Hollister,

California, half way to God-knows-where, watching the morning light on Sabine's pretty face as she sleeps.

I need a miracle.

Instead, there's a knock on the van window.

The sight startles me: An old man's sunburned face pressed to the window that's rolled open just an inch.

"What do you want?" Sabine mumbles as she wakes.

The old man shimmies his fingers into the open space and pushes the window down. He wants to warn us about Pacheco Pass, he says. "You taking Pacheco Pass?" He nods at us as he asks the question, like he already knows the answer. Like we're already on Pacheco Pass. "A lot of people die up there," he says. "On Pacheco Pass." The old man talks real slow, "a lot of people die," he says again and I have this sudden feeling that he intends to kill us before we have a chance to die up there, but pretty Sabine just shakes her head and she says, "Peace, man," and she fills the bowl of her purple water bong and she says, "Peace out, my kind man," and sort of shoes him away as she inhales the smoke and holds it in for a long time. And the man goes away and Sabine looks at me and exhales and smiles quick and finally asks, "What's it like?"

And I say, "What's *what* like?"

And she says, "What's it like not being very attractive?"

And I don't say anything.

But I kind of die up there. Pacheco Pass.

toxic

I don't think I've ever written about the house on Bryant Street. We probably only lived there for a couple of months. It was a strange little place, begging to be torn down and forgotten—a pale blue pre-fab duplex in a neighborhood full of beautiful old Victorians and 1920s Spanish revivals.

We rented it, were allowed to rent it somehow, the three of us—me and Mateo who were both fifteen or sixteen and still in high school, and Timothy who was older, maybe 22 or 23, which seemed very old to us.

So we rented it, were allowed to rent it.

It was just a few blocks from the Spanish house where my mom and John still lived.

I dragged the old round wooden table out of their garage and carried it to the house on Bryant Street and called that prefab duplex "home."

A man from the phone company came in his blue uniform and we got a phone. We got a phone number. We sat at the round wooden table and we wrote down our phone number and wrote down the corresponding letters from the keypad. We set to work trying to spell something and—miraculously—our phone number spelled UGLY.

You could call us at 321-UGLY.

You could call us if you needed pot or coke or speed or ecstasy.

You could call and talk to any one of us.

If you asked for Timothy, you could get heroin, too.

He was old. Timothy.

His girlfriend was a nurse at Stanford Hospital, so we had plenty of clean needles, too. We'd give you clean needles with your heroin.

It was the '80s, after all.

Timothy. His girlfriend didn't like me, didn't like that I shared a bedroom with her man.

What's the difference between reflection and memory?

I don't know.

I didn't know.

All I knew was that drugs were supposed to make you skinny, and I started putting on weight right away. I weighed 115 pounds, I weighed 120 pounds, I weighed 127 pounds, I weighed 132 pounds. I weighed 140 pounds.

"Jesus, I'm getting fat."

I'm in the kitchen now. In the kitchen of that pale blue prefab duplex on Bryant Street. I'm chopping carrots on a wooden cutting board, chopping green onions, chopping apples. At the health food store on University Avenue this morning a man told me I could cleanse myself with a salad of carrots and green onions and apples and raisins and lemon juice. "You're toxic," he said. "You look toxic to me."

I was toxic, all right.

I took a different drug every day. Like maybe I'd take speed on Monday, coke on Tuesday, ecstasy on Wednesday and Thursday, mushrooms on Friday if I didn't have to work, smoke pot on Saturday morning and wait to see what the weekend would bring.

I'd had the brilliant idea that I wouldn't get addicted to any one drug if I kept changing it up.

The house on Bryant Street. It smells like Winston cigarettes.
I drop ecstasy with Bunny Cho.
Smoke endless bong hits with Sabine.
Wait for things that never happen.

It's warm outside, and warm inside, the house on Bryant Street.

The sun streams in through the sliding glass doors that lead to a cement patio. The sun streams in and the dust dances in the golden spotlight. The dust is the star here.

If we have our own place, that makes us grown-ups, right?
We are fifteen and sixteen and 23.
Grown ups.
It's springtime.
My feet itch.

The house on Bryant Street where the cops come every Saturday night when we play Nina Hagen too loud, play David Bowie too loud, play James Taylor too loud, the house on Bryant Street.

I'm chopping apples.

It's midday on a Saturday. Maybe it's midday. Maybe we don't have a clock. Maybe Timothy will emerge from the bedroom soon. Maybe he won't.

I cut a lemon, squeeze the juice over my chopped salad.

A UPS delivery man arrives with a television. A strange gift from one of my mom's students on death row at San Quentin.

Mateo sits at the round wooden table that reminds me of my childhood; reminds me that I used to be a child.

I push play on the stereo. *Let it Be.*

"I can't believe you like the Beatles," Mateo says. He's loading his red plastic water bong.

I don't like the Beatles that much, but I don't correct him.

He's beautiful, Mateo, but there's something off about him. "The Beatles are so cheesy." He starts to sing, waving his arms and mocking the Beatles, "Oh, yeah, everything's gonna be all right.

Wonderful. Beautiful! No fucking problems for the Beatles! Don't need revolution! Status quo, oh yeah—" Mateo sucks the smoke from his bong and holds it in his chest for a long time. He exhales the mucky grey smoke with a cough. "It's weird," he says. "When you inhale the smoke it's white and when you exhale it's always grey."

"It's because you're toxic," I tell him.

And he laughs. He stands to put a Talking Heads album on the turntable.

He's depressed, Mateo. He's been depressed ever since the car accident that killed his twin brother and didn't kill him.

I'm depressed, too, but I don't know why. I can't point to some accident and say I wasn't depressed before that and now I am.

I spoon my cleansing salad concoction into two blue bowls. "I have an idea," I tell Mateo as I set his bowl in front of him at the table.

He squints at my salad and sniffs.

"I'm gonna drop out of high school," I say. "I'm gonna drop the fuck out."

Mateo picks up his fork. "Yeah, man," he says. "Tune in, turn on, drop out." He laughs at his own brilliance.

"I'm serious," I tell Mateo.

And he nods. "I'd do it, too," he says. "If I felt like doing anything." He laughs again, but there are tears in his eyes.

runaway

I ran away for a hundred reasons. I ran away for no reason. I ran away because I was bored. I ran away because I didn't want to become boring. I ran away because I was high. I ran away because I woke up sober and the first thing I saw was a bright and metaphorical window and some uncrazy voice in my head whispered: *This is your chance. Flee.*

California shone like some invincible summer; shines in me. We were carob-eaters, co-op shoppers, children of "non-sexist child-rearing." We were chain smokers, unbaptized Catholics, poets-in-the-making. But everyone in California had a secret, and secrets make you crazy.

I had secrets even from myself.

I ran away because everybody's story in California seemed to end up crazy. All of us perpetually hitchhiking to the mental hospital.

I ran away because I was afraid.

I ran away because I was becoming a cliché.

I ran away because everyone said I was too smart for my age but I had the vague idea that this intellectual intelligence wouldn't help me much in the world. Just because you're smart doesn't mean you have sense. It doesn't mean you have experience. It doesn't mean you're not, well—sixteen.

And so you're sixteen.

You run away.

You leave a note on the table: *Yours sincerely in wood-life.*

You're sixteen and you run away with your backpack and your Sony Walkman and your extra pair of jeans and your *Lonely Planet* travel guide and your black hardbound sketchbook—*Stories by Ariel Gore.*

You run.

You *fly.*

You're all courage and faith. You're all under-confidence and "Don't take my picture, I don't like my face."

You're fearless. And you're the perfect embodiment of fear.

You've been reading Hermann Hesse and Alan Watts and so you go east. Of course you go east. You've been studying Chinese. You want to become a Buddhist, a communist. You're looking for lost cities. You are looking not to become a cliché.

But of course you know: It's already too late.

the bar in hong kong

The bar in Hong Kong is supposed to be British-themed, Djuna tells me. Friar Tuck's.
Outside, there's a big wooden statue of Friar Tuck. But the theme ends there. Inside, it looks like any other Hong Kong hot spot. Dark, with lava lamps glowing from low, black tables. Tourists and businessmen and locals who swear they're going to school in Canada come fall; Girls with Minnie Mouse purses and girls with Louis Vuitton purses.

I get the job easily. A five-minute interview standing at the bar. Just like Djuna said.

Djuna. I met her at the youth hostel on Nathan Road. She knows things, Djuna. She has curly red hair and freckles on her nose.

Back at the youth hostel, Djuna loans me her book on making cocktails. "Pink ladies and grasshoppers are what the chicks order," she says. "The guys drink Jack. Jack neat. Jack up. Jack straight. Jack rocks. Jack soda."

"A pink lady is gin, grenadine, heavy cream, and cracked ice. A grasshopper is crème de menthe, crème de cacao, heavy cream, and cracked ice. Neat means right out of the bottle. Up means you shake it with ice to chill it, but strain the ice and serve it looking neat. Straight up should mean up, but with whiskey it usually means neat. Rocks are ice cubes. Soda is soda. Pretty simple. Still, you have to know how to make everything—just in case. You have to read the book."

I read the book. I know how to make everything.

"You have nice legs," the guy who interviewed me tells me on my first day.

I'm wearing the required mini skirt and Polo top. "Uh," I hesitate. "Thanks."

"We share all the tips," he tells me. "Put them in this box and you'll get your share at the end of the week."

I'm about to tell him that forced tip-sharing is illegal, but then I remember it's probably not illegal in Hong Kong and anyway I don't have a work visa.

"Yeah," Djuna tells me back at the hostel. "That's just the way Jimmy is. You'll get used to him."

I make pink ladies and grasshoppers. They look like watery Boardwalk milk shakes. The girls with Minnie Mouse purses order the pink ladies. The Louis Vuitton girls order the grasshoppers. There's no telling the men apart, really. White or Chinese, they all look like Jimmy. They're tourists and businessmen and locals who swear they're going to school in Canada come fall. It's like Djuna said. They order Jack.

china

China isn't so romantic after all. China isn't pink cherry blossoms and happy communist children in their school uniforms all waving at me and smiling. China isn't stunning, jagged mountains and salty, delicious plates of noodles. China isn't mystical *Journey to the East* by Hermann Hesse. China isn't lost cities I stumble upon in transcendental dreaming.

China is grey skies and grey cityscapes, hard work and hard silences.

China is laughing at me, China is pointing.

I am determined to love China, but my determination is waning.

A week, a month, a season, a year.

China is still pointing at me, wagging her finger and calling me fat, calling me "white ghost girl."

I don't know where I am. I don't know why I stay here.

I thought I would come to China and step into the pages of *National Geographic*. I thought I would come to China and become a real communist.

My noodles don't smell good.

The sounds of construction and earth-moving machines are loud outside my window.

I catch another train.

expecting

We live in squats that smell of rain and apples. We talk late into the nights, the Clash always playing on someone's boom box.

In the mornings, Lance steals baguettes for our breakfast and makes unfiltered coffee on a camping stove and we smoke unfiltered cigarettes.

"She's lived in China," Lance brags to anyone who will listen, but we're in Amsterdam now. We're in London now. We're in Paris now.

Rain and apples.

When the skies begin to clear in springtime, we pack up our extra pair of jeans, pull our leather jackets on over our T-shirts, tie flannel shirts around our waists, and head south to pay our respects to Sara-la-Kali, patron saint of the Gypsies. In a small French town, crowds of people meander toward the beach. They carry candles and sing songs to the three Saint Marys, and to Sara-la-Kali. A long procession to the shore. We follow the Gypsies and the tourists. We smoke and we drink.

"God is here," Lance whispers, and I know he's right. The Goddess Sara-la-Kali.

I wake under grey blankets at the shore, a young woman nudging my arm. "Do you know how to build a fire?" she wants to know.

I sit up slowly, take in the salty morning air and all the people camped out in tents or sleeping bags or wool blankets.

The young woman wears baggy jeans and a thin sweatshirt, her dark hair tied in a messy bun.

"I used to know how," I offer, "I can try to help." We gather driftwood and scraps of newspaper, use too many matches to get the thing going. The woman looks Indian and Eastern European at the same time. "Are you a Gypsy?" I ask.

"By blood," she says. "But obviously not by lifestyle. I grew up in London. I'm studying Romani history at university."

"That's cool. So—is Sara-la-Kali Catholic or Hindu?"

"Both," the woman says. "The Gypsies came from India, originally, but lots of them are Catholics now. Saint Sara is the Catholic incarnation of the Hindu goddess Kali." She warms her hands over the fire. "Are you expecting?" she asks.

"What do you mean?"

She shrugs. "You're obviously terribly thin, but you have that glow about you. As if you're expecting? A child? Of course you know, sometimes when people are travelers, well, they come and they ask Saint Sara-la-Kali to bless their children."

I warm my hands over the fire and think about that. *Expecting*.

Part Three:
A Quick Brush of Wings

(Just two stories, actually, salvaged from
the wreckage of a bunch of '90s stories)

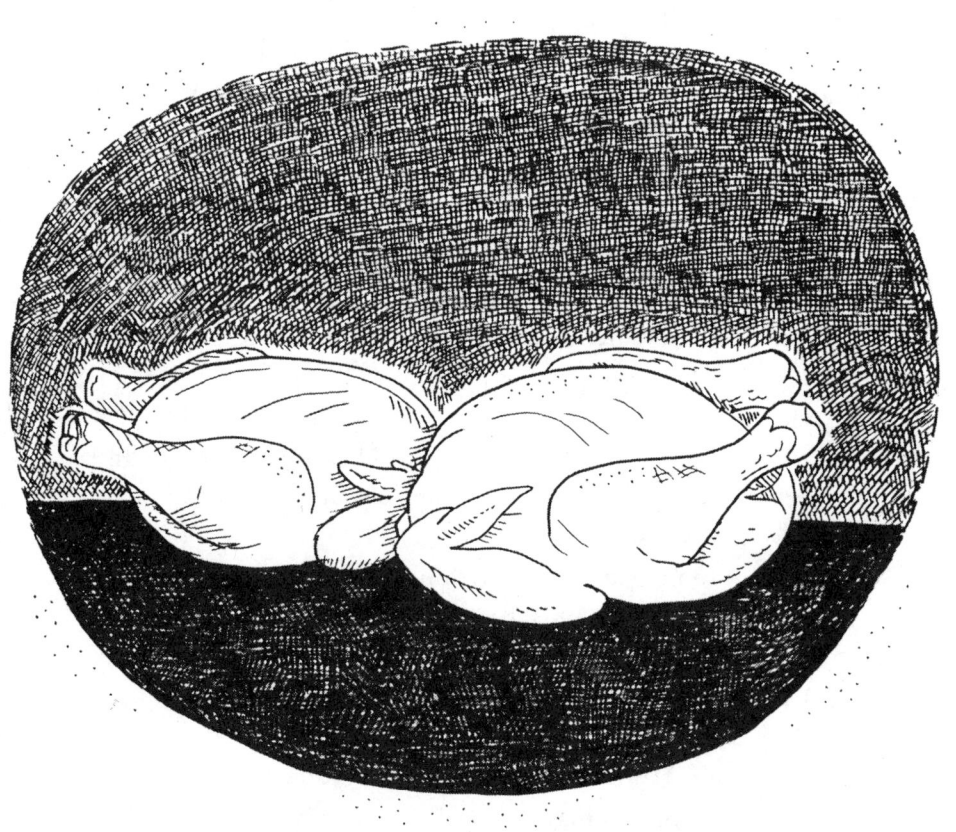

counselor

I don't like those people who tell kids that adolescence is the best years of our lives.
That's a lie.
That's the kind of lie that can really kill you. The kind of lie that makes you feel alone in your depression. The kind of lie that can scare you for a long time.
There were other lies like that.

"I think I want to be a writer," I'd told the career counselor at the junior college where I almost signed up for classes.
I sat across from her in her little brown office. She wore a little brown suit.
She shook her head when I said that and she laughed a quiet and bitter laugh and she let the corners of her mouth turn up into a sneer. Her voice fell an octave when she answered me: "Good luck," is what she said.
I just sat there. I didn't say anything. I glanced over at my baby, asleep in her little blue polka-dotted umbrella stroller.
The counselor sort of leaned back in her plush brown chair then and adjusted her brown jacket and tilted her head to the side like she was maybe trying to pop a vertebrae in her neck and she said, "Miss Gore." And then she looked down at the piece of paper in front of her, maybe trying to remember my name. And

she said, "Ariel." She said, "Miss Gore, you have a child to take care of now." She said, "You really ought to make an attempt to come down to earth and think about that. You need to think about your child and ask yourself how you're going to make a living."

I was nineteen.

I nodded a few times too many.

I stood up slow.

Her words made my heart contract, but I still felt compelled to be polite. "Thank you," I said before I grabbed the handles of the umbrella stroller.

I pushed the stroller.

I let myself out of that dumb brown office.

I pushed the stroller.

My pace quickened as I walked away, as I pushed.

My mother's words rattle around in my head, too. "You chose this life, Ariel. You're on your own." Like I'm 19 and I already made my bed.

The cement path led past the pillars, past the little gardens, toward a green expanse. My walk morphed into a run. Hot tears streamed down my face. I pushed the stroller. The baby slept. She kept on sleeping. I felt like an idiot for telling that woman what I wanted, what I wanted to be. I felt like an idiot for wanting something I had no right to want. For thinking I could do something.

I didn't know how to live, that counselor was right. I didn't know how to make a living.

Writer. What a joke.

a quick brush of wings

If I wanted to be a writer, I realized, I would have to go where the writers were.
  I had to find these people.
These writers.
I had to seek them out and be in their presence and inhale the air they exhaled.
I had to learn from them.
And here was my chance. I saw the ad in the local alternative weekly: *An evening with Anne Lamott and Amy Tan.* These were maybe the two most powerful thirty-something or forty-something women in the San Francisco literary scene. *Anne Lamott and Amy Tan.* They would be my foremothers, my teachers. If only I could share this evening with them. Yes.
I *had* to be there, obviously.
Fort Mason Center in San Francisco.
$150 per person.
I hardly ever drove into the city.
It meant getting Lance to watch the baby. He'd come to California now, too. He lived four blocks from us, was suing me for custody.
It meant the gas and the bridge toll.
It meant tapping the dashboard three times and praying that the Dodge would make it. This time, it also meant $150.

$150. Just over a quarter of my monthly income.

But what was $150, really? What was a quarter tank of gas and a quarter of my monthly income and a $3 bridge toll when it would make me a writer?

I would meet these women and they would see me—they would see the writer in me and they would lean into me and they would whisper the secrets that writers whisper.

The ad—even seeing that ad—had been destiny. Clearly. I hardly ever read that weekly paper.

I had $21 in the cookie jar for my gas and electricity bill. I only needed another $129 for the ticket. The gas and electric company could wait. If we had to live in the dark for a week or three weeks—what did it matter? This evening was the thing that mattered. *An evening with Anne Lamott and Amy Tan.*

I showed the ad to Mary, the old woman who'd recently moved into my neighborhood in Petaluma. I bounced Maia on my knee as I opened the newspaper on Mary's Formica kitchen table. I pointed. "Anne Lamott and Amy Tan," I hummed. I'd been helping Mary around her little government apartment, putting away groceries for her, pulling weeds in her tiny front garden. We'd shared Christmas dinner. I'd invited her over after the man from the food bank called to tell me I was eligible for a free turkey. When I went to pick it up, it turned out to be two chickens—they'd run out of turkeys. But I had some vegetables in the fridge, so I made chicken soup for Christmas dinner and I didn't skim off the fat. Chicken soup for me and Mary and the baby. We sat in the little dining alcove in my apartment, and she told me this and that about her life. She was Athabaskan Indian, she said. Born up in Alaska but her mother died of tuberculosis and she was adopted out to a white family down in Seattle.

Mary. She had short, black hair and laughing eyes. She looked at the ad for the evening with the writers and said, "sounds like a lot of money."

But what did Mary know?
She was poor, she was old.
I knew what I had to do.
It was a clear-sky day in Petaluma.
I got Lance to watch the baby.
I used my bill money for the gas and the bridge.
Tom Waits sang "Hang on St. Christopher" on my car radio.
I used the rent money for the ticket.

Amy Tan read something unpublished and showed slides of her grandparents.

Anne Lamott said she'd been a black-belt codependent and had just broken up with a man who wasn't fit to drink her bath water.

Afterwards, the writers drank punch around a table and people approached them and told them they loved their work and told them they'd changed their lives and told them they liked the talks they'd just given.

I stood against a wall and watched.

I stood against a wall and watched the light change as the sun set over the bay.

I stood against a wall and bit my fingernails.

I cried at Mary's kitchen table the next morning, cried at what an idiot I'd been. The rain poured outside, flooding the streets and walkways. I would never be a writer, it was true. That counselor in her drab brown office back at the junior college had been right. *What was I thinking?* I had to come down to earth. This wet earth. I had to figure out how to make a living. I had to figure out how to live. I had a *child* to take care of.

Mary just smiled at me, shook her head the way she did. "Ariel," she said. "You *are* with the writers. Right now and right here you're with the writers. And here we're doing the things that writers do. We're washing the dishes and we're putting away the groceries. We're helping each other. We're paying attention, aren't we?"

I thought she was sweet, old Athabaskan Mary, but obviously she was kind of doddery. Helping Mary around her apartment was all good and fine, but it was hardly where the writers were. And I wanted to be a *writer*. My mind wandered. I was back at Fort Mason. Back with the writers and thinking of all the things I might have said to them if I wasn't so afraid. If they had looked at me.

"I have something for you," Mary said, interrupting my writer-thought. She stood up, left me there to breathe in my self-pity.

A few minutes later she came back with a slim volume. *A Quick Brush of Wings* by Mary TallMountain. "My new book," she said. "I've been meaning to give you a copy."

I looked at the title and I looked at the author's name for a long time before I let it sink in.

Mary.

TallMountain.

And with that Mary leaned into me and she whispered the secrets that writers whisper. And I breathed her in and I became one.

thank you

Lipstick-kiss thank yous to everyone who helped make this book possible. My editors and co-conspiritors: Dexter Flowers, Krystee Sidwell, Lani Jo Leigh, Sailor Holladay, Maria Fabulosa, Lisa Sinnett and all the Wayward Writers. And to my generous Kickstarter project backers: the lovely Lotti Pharriss Knowles, Rachel Ford, Valerie Wagner, Kait Moon, Martine Habib, Vitali Rozynko, Mary Willimas, Diana Rempe, Caitlin Bechtel, Flore Cuny, Melissa Green, Erin Edmundon, Catherine DeLuca, Anne Jonas, and so many more. I hope you enjoyed the stories. Surely we will meet again soon!

about ariel & summer

ARIEL GORE is the founding editor of *Hip Mama* and the author of seven books including *Atlas of the Human Heart* and *How to Become a Famous Writer Before You're Dead*. She teaches writing online, in New Mexico, and in Portland, Oregon. You can write to her at 5 Bisbee Ct. 109-21, Santa Fe, NM, 87508 or you can find her online at http://arielgore.com.

SUMMER PIERRE ("yes, my parents were hippies") is the creator of the zine *Forgive Me* and the author of *The Artist in the Office: How to Thrive and Survive Seven Days a Week* and *Great Gals: Inspired Ideas for Living a Kick Ass Life*. She grew up in the San Francisco Bay Area and lives with her family in Brooklyn. You can find her online at http://summerpierre.com.